Existentialism

A Beginner's Guide

D0967167

ONEWORLD BEGINNER'S GUIDES combine an original, inventive, and engaging approach with expert analysis on subjects ranging from art and history to religion and politics, and everything in between. Innovative and affordable, books in the series are perfect for anyone curious about the way the world works and the big ideas of our time.

Existentialism
A Beginner's Guide

Thomas E. Wartenberg

ONEWORLD

OXFORD

142.78
WAR

A Oneworld Book

Published by Oneworld Publications 2008

ISBN 978–1–85168–593–6

Typeset by Jayvee, Trivandrum, India
Cover design by Simon McFadden
Printed and bound in Great Britain by
TJ International Ltd, Padstow, Cornwall

Oneworld Publications
185 Banbury Road
Oxford OX2 7AR
England
www.oneworld-publications.com

Learn more about Oneworld. Join our mailing list to
find out about our latest titles and special offers at:

www.oneworld-publications.com

For the Whartons
In memory of Heinz, Nellie,
and Connie and for Peter
for first supporting my existential leanings
and
In memory of Joseph Epstein,
who first rekindled the flame

Contents

Preface

My interest in philosophy must have predated my receipt of Jean-Paul Sartre's *Being and Nothingness* one Christmas from my cousins, the Whartons. I suspect their gift was a response to my discovery of Walter Kaufmann's anthology, *Existentialism from Dostoevsky to Sartre*, in a bookstore during one of my weekly jaunts into Manhattan. I still have no idea why I chose to buy that particular book nor what cultural message might already have provoked an interest in its subject matter. I do know that I subsequently read a variety of essays, novels, stories, and plays as a result of making the Existentialists' acquaintance through that book, and that these works had a deep effect on me. Yet, in spite of my explorations, *Being and Nothingness* sat on my shelf for years – unread. Only when I began to teach a course on Existentialism did I actually pull Sartre's masterpiece off the shelf and attempt to plumb its depths.

Despite my reluctance to read one of its most important philosophical texts, Existentialism had a big impact on me as an alienated teenager growing up in the suburbs of New York in the 1950s and 1960s. It helped me interpret my feelings of isolation and loneliness as reflective of more than my own psyche, and furthered my understanding of what seemed to me a superficial, materialist world of upper-middle-class opulence surrounding me. Novels of alienated youths and essays pointing out life's absurdity struck a chord in my soul that continues to vibrate to this day.

My entrance into professional philosophy, however, proceeded along a very different route. A course taught by

Joseph Epstein provoked my interest in questions posed in the philosophy of science, for I recognized a shared concern with Existentialism about understanding reality, despite fundamental differences in how that concern was addressed. My hope is that Joe would have found this book a valuable contribution for making the Existentialists' approach to answering life's essential questions accessible to analytical minds like his own.

As my familiarity with the world of philosophy increased, the subject of Existentialism was never one I felt compelled to address. No course that I took in aesthetics or epistemology, the history of philosophy or ethics, ever included writings by any of the Existentialists. Indeed, because American graduate schools are dominated by the Analytic tradition, there was even a somewhat snobbish sense that Existentialism was not really philosophy in *our* sense of the word, but more of a popular form of writing that merely imitated deep thought.

It was only when I was asked to teach a course on Existentialism that I rediscovered my original attraction to that form of philosophical thinking. The Existentialists then exerted their pull on me a second time, pushing me towards a more public conception of philosophy than that endorsed by many contemporary philosophers, one I have remained committed to ever since. One of the attractions of writing a book about Existentialism is that the philosophers who are brought together under the term articulate a view of the nature of philosophy that sees philosophy less as an academic specialty than as a broad cultural practice. This practice is oriented toward a reflection on and an assessment of the nature of the lives we live and the society in which we live them. In fact, few of the thinkers I shall be writing about held an academic position. Beginning with Friedrich Nietzsche, thinkers in the Existentialist tradition rejected the professorial life, perhaps fearing that following this profession would hinder their ability to express their views freely.

Another attraction of writing a book about the Existentialists is the wide appeal their ideas have had to people the world over. Just as the Existentialists were able to reach me as a teen, they continue to help people in vastly different circumstances confront some of their most basic concerns about life and death, which I feel are underappreciated in today's philosophical environment. Exploring what it means to be a human being living in the world through their plays, stories, and novels, the Existentialists took their philosophy into the public sphere. But when one moves beyond these more popular literary forms to the specifically *philosophical* essays and books that the Existentialists produced, one is met by a difficulty. Because the Existentialists articulated their ideas through a criticism of their philosophical predecessors, they employ such an abstract and rarified philosophical vocabulary that it can be difficult to understand precisely what they are saying. It often may seem as if they are employing an obscure and enigmatic code that there is no way to crack.

My goal in writing this book is to reveal the excitement and allure of Existentialism in such a way that even my own teenage self – and thus everyone who has found the Existentialists' ideas useful but hard to comprehend – can grasp them. Whether I have succeeded, of course, is not for me to say.

* * *

There are many people who have helped me in innumerable ways in the writing of this book. First, my editors at Oneworld Publications deserve special thanks: Martha Jay, for first broaching to me the idea of writing the book, and Marsha Filion for bringing the project to fruition with so much care, concern, and intelligence. Without their support and guidance, this book would never have been written.

My students in Philosophy 255 – Existentialism – have been a constant inspiration to me over the years. Their interest in and enthusiasm for Existentialism is one of the main reasons that I have continued to teach the subject. Since my students also helped me to see that the ideas of the Existentialists could be expressed much more clearly than they originally were, my commitment to writing a book like this owes a great deal to them.

A number of people have commented on different parts of this manuscript. Bill de Vries, my former graduate school colleague and friend ever since, did me the great service of reading an early version of the manuscript and saving me from many errors. Ed Royce, a former colleague and dear friend, was an excellent interlocutor with whom I could discuss my ideas on this school of philosophy. His comments on specific chapters were invaluable. My colleague and friend, Gary Matthews, also read the manuscript and made many important suggestions. I also want to thank my good friend and sometime colleague, Sean Sayers, for reading and commenting on the penultimate version of the manuscript. The manuscript has also benefited from the suggestions and comments of an anonymous reader. Finally, thanks to Reisa Alexander for editorial assistance and Eva Goodwin for help with the Filmography.

One of my friends and intellectual colleagues – Alan Schiffmann – deserves special acknowledgment. I had the good fortune to spend a summer reading and talking about Martin Heidegger's *Being and Time* with Alan, and our mutual excitement at realizing the significance of his Existentialist critique of traditional philosophy helped deepen my appreciation of the entire school of thought. This book bears testimony to the significant role that Alan played in the maturation of my own philosophical thought. I hope he can find in this book traces of our conversations that summer, now nearly twenty years ago.

A big nod of thanks to my son and computer technician, Jake. Without his timely assistance, this book would have remained merely virtual.

Finally, I want to acknowledge the huge debt I owe to my wife, Wendy Berg, for her caring love and support over the years. Feminist economists have been pointing out for some time that women work in ways that are not only unpaid but also unrecognized. This holds true of Wendy and all the ways in which her toil has assisted my own intellectual activity. She has been that silent presence behind the scenes without whom I would not have been able to accomplish whatever I have. For doing all that she has for me – and for her love – I am so very grateful that I can only acknowledge my own good fortune in having her as my life's partner.

★ ★ ★

I shall end this preface with a few notes about the language used in this book. First, a note on gender: the masculinized language of many of the Existentialists calls for some comment. On the one hand, one is tempted to view a claim like '*man's* essence is freedom' as simply a sexist way of making a general point about human beings. Accepting this point of view would allow me to simply note this use of the masculine gender as an unfortunate tendency among the primarily male Existentialists and then move on. But, as was pointed out by Simone de Beauvoir, the lone woman and feminist in the Existentialist tradition about whom I shall write, there is more to this linguistic practice than its use of the masculine term as the generic one, for it involves an implicit and illicit valorization and universalization of *men's* traits as the norms for the species as a whole. Writers adopt various strategies to call attention to this deeply problematic usage. Mine consists of this note and a sustained attempt to keep my own prose sex and gender neutral, except when a more specific use is intended. Although flagging each sexist usage with a '*sic*' once appealed to me, I now find it irritating for its elevation of the writer's consciousness over and above the 'unfortunate' thinker who was, by implication, trapped within a sexist point of view.

Second, a comment about Eurocentrism: philosophy is not the exclusive property of European cultures and those, such as that of the United States, derived from it. It is, nonetheless, important to recognize that Existentialism developed as a movement within European and European-influenced philosophy. For convenience, I refer to this type of philosophy as 'Western.' Consequently, when the word 'philosophy' stands alone in this book, it should be read more correctly as 'Western philosophy.' Felicity of style has led me to drop it often enough that it is necessary for me to issue this warning.

Finally, a comment on translation and terminology. The concept of *being*, a *nominalization* of the verb 'to be,' figures prominently in this book, as it does in the writings of the Existentialists. In English, 'existence' is a synonym for 'being.' Either word can be used to translate the words used by the Existentialists, *Sein* (German) and *être* (French). Generally, 'being' is used in the translations of German philosophers such as Heidegger while 'existence' is used for those of French philosophers such as Sartre. This can lead to unnecessary confusion when the two nationalities are considered together, as they are in this book. So just remember that 'being' and 'existence' are simply two ways of saying the same thing. Similarly, we can refer to a thing as either a 'being' or an 'existent' without altering our meaning. It will be important to bear these synonymous usages in mind, although I will occasionally make this equivalence explicit by placing one of the two words in parentheses.

And now, to echo the cry that animated philosophers in this tradition, *on to the things themselves*, the ideas of the Existentialists!

Introduction

'To be, or not to be, that is the question' (*Hamlet* III, i, 56).
These words, uttered by the eponymous Prince of Denmark in
Shakespeare's play, are so famous and have been parodied so
often that it is hard for us to actually focus on what they say. Yet,
once we consider them more closely, we realize that Hamlet is
having what we now would call an *existential crisis*: should he go
on living or simply end it all? The question of suicide, which
Albert Camus – one of the leading figures in the Existentialist
Tradition – viewed as 'the one truly serious philosophical
problem,' is one that many people have faced at least once in
their lives. The Existentialists' concern with this issue is one
reason why Existentialism has remained such a vibrant form of
philosophical thought, for it takes this question seriously,
seeking to guide people's reflections on this vexing life-issue in
a manner that helps them not only clarify their own feelings
and ideas, but also avoid simplistic solutions and their dire
consequences.

But let's not leave Hamlet too quickly for the heady realm of
Existentialist philosophy. Why, exactly, does Hamlet contemplate suicide? Because killing himself appears to be the only
solution to his inability to take decisive action and avenge his
father's murder. Through the aid of his father's ghost, Hamlet
has discovered that his uncle, Claudius, killed his father and
married his mother. Given the conventions of his day, Hamlet
must avenge his father's wrongful murder by killing Claudius.
Yet Hamlet hesitates. Here is how we can summarize his
thought process: 'Should I do it or should I not? Well, certainly
not when he's praying, because that would send him to heaven.

When then? I'm not sure. Maybe I'm just a wretched son for not avenging my father's death quickly enough!' Eventually Hamlet decides that suicide may be the only answer to his quandary, the only way out of his dilemma. So, he begins his famous soliloquy by raising the issue. But, even then, he hesitates: 'It's too scary to kill myself,' runs the gist of his reflection, 'because I don't know what will happen to me after I die. Maybe I should be really, really sure that Claudius is the murderer before I act. I know. I'll put on a play and see how he reacts …' Hamlet, we realize, has trouble doing the very thing he knows he must. But why is that?

From the point of view of Existentialism, Hamlet's inability to act decisively reflects a fundamental aspect of the human condition: The very thing that makes us unique among the vast array of things that exist in the world – *our freedom* – is also our biggest burden. The problem with being free, the Existentialists point out, is that it forces us to take complete responsibility for what we do or fail to do. If I am free to do something or to refrain from doing it, then whether I do it or not is totally up to me. Once I have acted, I can't pin the blame on anyone or anything else. Yet, at crucial moments in our lives, this responsibility can seem absolutely overwhelming. On the one hand, our ability to control our own fates feels intoxicating, for we realize we have the ability to take action in the world and, in so doing, remake it according to our own design. On the other hand, we can be completely intimidated by what that very ability entails, for, once we act, what we have done cannot be undone. This latter realization results in our experiencing anxiety, as we face the burden of having to make a free choice. And this is exactly what causes Hamlet's dilemma: he knows that he must avenge his father's death, but he cannot accept the responsibility that doing so brings with it.

At the heart of Shakespeare's great play, then, lies an insight into the human condition that is central to the philosophical movement known as Existentialism. We humans are not as keen about our own freedom as many people, philosophers included, have suggested. Indeed, the word 'freedom' now often seems to function as a shorthand way of talking about all that is good and valuable in human life. Yet, what the Existentialists realized – and in so doing made philosophically respectable an idea that can be found in literature at least as far back as Shakespeare – was that we are constituted as a species with a deep-seated ambivalence toward our own freedom. A fundamental aim of this book is to show how significant this insight is and how it structured one of the most important philosophical movements of the nineteenth and twentieth centuries.

Now, the Existentialists make up a pretty unusual 'school' of philosophy. Just one philosopher commonly regarded as an Existentialist, Jean-Paul Sartre, accepted this label as a suitable way of characterizing his philosophical stance. Others – such as Martin Heidegger – explicitly rejected the term. Only in post-World War II France did a number of the thinkers we now group together as Existentialists take themselves to be members of a unified philosophical school. But even in Paris, this unity was fragile and was soon fractured. Perhaps, this is reflective of the fact that the Existentialists disagree with one another, at least in part, on virtually every philosophical issue imaginable. Take the existence of God. While there are many atheistic Existentialists such as Camus and Sartre, there are also religious Existentialists such as Søren Kierkegaard, the nineteenth-century Danish theologian and philosopher. Does this mean that it is a mistake to lump together this motley crew of thinkers?

No. For despite these differences, it remains important to realize that this group of philosophers shares a unique intellectual outlook. In exploring the nature of Existentialism, I will therefore bring together philosophers from such diverse settings as nineteenth-century Denmark and Paris in the aftermath of World War II, the time and place of Existentialism's 'heyday.' My aim in so doing is not only to develop an understanding of the Existentialists' unique philosophical perspective, but also to demonstrate that it remains a viable outlook to this day.

My exposition of Existentialism will take place by introducing the core ideas of this philosophical tradition. In this way, I will be able cautiously and carefully to guide you through the difficult shoals of the Existentialists' reflections about the fundamental meaning of our lives and existence. So although I will discuss the major figures in the Existentialist Tradition – Søren Kierkegaard, Friedrich Nietzsche, Martin Heidegger, Jean-Paul Sartre, Maurice Merleau-Ponty, and Albert Camus – and two more thinkers who deserve to enter such a pantheon but are often ignored – Simone de Beauvoir and Frantz Fanon – I will not do so in the usual way of presenting their ideas in historical sequence. Not only will this enable us to see the fundamental unity underlying the different theories of the Existentialist philosophers, it will also allow me to present Existentialism as a living philosophy. Just as God seems to have survived Nietzsche's proclamation of his death in the late nineteenth century, Existentialism retains its vitality as a way of thinking about human life even though many, including both logical positivists and post-modernists, have prophesied its impending death. My goal is to make the living, breathing tradition of Existentialism more readily available as a philosophical perspective on our lives as finite human beings. To do so, I will discuss the major contributions the Existentialists have made to our understanding of the nature of human existence.

Perhaps it will be useful for me to explain why I think Existentialism should be seen as a viable alternative on the current marketplace of philosophical theories rather than as an outmoded form of thought developed in the cafés of post-war Paris by Gauloise-smoking poseurs. Existentialism is arguably the only contemporary form of philosophy that remains true to the conception of philosophy first articulated over two and a half millennia ago in Ancient Greece. For the Greeks, philosophy was not, initially anyway, something to be studied in isolation by a group of specialists, but rather the expression of a way of life, a mode of conduct. As a result, the Greeks believed that philosophy had to address the most basic questions that human beings face about their lives – Why am I here? How should I live my life? What significance does death have for me? – in a way that would resonate with how people actually confront these problems in their daily lives. The fact that we now refer to these questions as *existential* ones is testimony to the ongoing relevance of Existentialism to the essential difficulties we face as human beings, even those of us living at the beginning of the twenty-first century. Indeed, one might even maintain that Existentialism attempts to restore philosophy to its ancient mission of exploring the fundamental dilemmas that human beings face during the course of their lives.

It is important to note that I have formulated these questions in the first-person singular, rather than plural: 'Why am *I* here?' rather than 'Why are *we* here?' This is indicative of an important belief shared by the Existentialists: that *individuality* is a fundamental value of human life. Indeed, this emphasis on the individual human being is one of the features that unites all the divergent Existentialist thinkers. What the Existentialists sought to counter was the tendency of human beings to live their lives guided by standards valid for all; what they advocated instead was the attempt by each of us to structure a life in a way that embodies what is distinctive about us as an individual. Rather than submit to the norms of what has been called 'the mass,' 'the herd,' and 'the crowd,' the Existentialists encourage people to develop their uniqueness, their own special qualities. This means that the answers people develop to the fundamental questions about how to live their lives are ones that they have to work out as individuals. Hence, the Existentialists' distrust of the general and their admiration for the particular.

Another characteristic of Existentialism that sets it apart from other schools of philosophy is that the Existentialists used different media to communicate their ideas. While most of the central Existentialists wrote those weighty and abstract tomes recognizable to all as 'philosophy' – titles such as *Being and Time* and *Being and Nothingness* signal the abstruse nature of these texts – they also wrote in a wide variety of other forms that they took to be equally important means for conveying their worldview. Sartre's play, *No Exit*, is still produced the world over, and Camus's novel, *The Stranger*, continues to introduce young people to some of the basic ideas of Existentialism. Maybe because of this, there are also many contemporary plays and novels as well as movies and even comic strips that embody Existentialist thinking. So, not only did such canonical writers such as Fyodor Dostoevsky and Franz Kafka make important contributions to Existentialist thought, but we also find traces of the movement in popular culture, as in the name of the band, The Exies, and in films such as *Stranger than Fiction* (2006) and *Donnie Darko* (2001). For this reason, as I discuss the philosophical claims of the Existentialist thinkers, I will draw on pop culture as well as traditional literary and philosophical works to illuminate the central claims of Existentialism.

Let me conclude my introduction with a suggestion: as you read *Existentialism: A Beginner's Guide*, think of it as a type of travel guide. Although there are entries about the history of the area we will be visiting, the main focus of the guide is the foremost tourist attractions, those features of the area that entice you to pay a visit. Later, once you have taken this guided tour, I hope you will come back to explore the 'sights' more thoroughly.

During our tour of the land of Existentialism, it is crucial to understand what is so important about this unusual approach toward the big questions we face in living our lives. So let's begin chapter 1 with a visit to the area's first big attraction: Existentialism's emphasis on the distinctive nature of being a *human* being.

1

Existence

> Even if man were nothing but a piano key, even if this were proved to him by natural science and mathematics, even then he would not become reasonable, but would purposely do something perverse out of sheer ingratitude, simply to have his own way ... then, after all, perhaps only by his curse will he attain his object, that is, really convince himself that he is a man and not a piano key! If you say that all this, too, can be calculated and tabulated ... then man would purposely go mad in order to be rid of reason and have his own way.
>
> (*Notes from Underground*, 28)

These words, uttered by the Underground Man, the narrator of Fyodor Dostoevsky's (see text box, p. 8) short novel, *Notes from Underground*, present one fundamental thesis of Existentialism: that human beings value their freedom more than anything else. The Underground Man says that freedom is so important to humans that we would prefer to go insane rather than accept the idea that our actions are completely determined by scientific laws. Although Dostoevsky's prose conveys the point more dramatically than your average Existentialist philosophical text, it clearly presents the Existentialist espousal of freedom as a fundamental characteristic of human beings, indeed the feature that most clearly makes us the unique creatures we are.

But where does the need for such a striking defense of human freedom come from? Written in 1864, *Notes from Underground* was a response to the threat that the natural sciences posed to human beings' self-understanding, for science claims to

> **Fyodor Mikhailovich Dostoevsky** (1821–1881) was one of the most important Russian novelists of the nineteenth century and arguably one of the greatest novelists of all time. As a young man, he was involved in radical politics and even served time in prison as a result of his seditious activities. Yet, after a firing squad pretended to carry out his death sentence in a mock execution, he became a conservative Christian.
>
> Despite his Christian beliefs, Dostoevsky was cognizant of the struggles involved in maintaining faith in the face of a world that appears not to justify it. Although his fictional writings make a case for adopting a religious worldview, his portraits of those who were tempted to reject that perspective have been very influential within the Existential Tradition, for, in depicting those unbelievers, Dostoevsky presented some of the basic arguments of Existentialism. His novels include *Notes from Underground* (1864), *Crime and Punishment* (1866), *The Idiot* (1869), *The Possessed* (1872), and *The Brothers Karamazov* (1880), the greatest of them all.

have the ability to explain everything that takes place in the world on the basis of its own natural laws. Dostoevsky structured his novel around the realization that science's bold pretense to have the capacity to understand and predict all occurrences constituted a deep crisis for human beings and their sense of themselves. Are we human beings no more than piano keys, whose every motion is completely determined by natural laws? Many people in the mid-nineteenth century were not willing to cede their own being, their own freedom, to the dictates of scientists. Especially in the aftermath of the French Revolution of 1789, freedom became the watchword of liberal intellectuals the world over, and it continues to be to this day. As the chains of monarchies and feudalism were broken through evolution and revolution, the bell of political freedom sounded throughout Europe and the Americas. Could all these upheavals have been merely the working out of natural laws instead of the result of human beings' innate capacity to structure their lives according to their own lights?

But what exactly is that freedom about which I have been writing and the Existentialists have so much to say? There are many types of freedom that philosophers have distinguished. We will only consider two. First, there is *social and political freedom*. Because human beings must interact with one another, they have developed a set of social conventions and political institutions to regulate their relationships. When freedom is talked about in this context, it indicates that these conventions and institutions must not illegitimately constrain the human beings who are governed by them. The claim is that people have an inherent right to determine the course of their own lives, so there needs to be a specific justification for limiting their choices in any way. This is a far cry from the structure of traditional societies, for the people living in them are generally born into specific social roles that they will occupy for their entire lives. Western democracies are intended to give their members the freedom to choose how to live their lives.

Underlying this social notion of freedom, however, there is a different, *metaphysical* concept of freedom. This is the sense of freedom that the Underground Man has in mind. The ancient Greek philosopher Aristotle (384–322 BCE) was the first to discuss it in any detail. To grasp what it is, think about a tennis ball. The ball coming at you across the net is not free. Its trajectory is determined by the laws of physics together with what physicists call 'initial conditions': how hard your opponent struck it, what direction it began moving in, whether there is wind, and so on. And the racket that you are going to hit it with is not free either, for it can only move if you swing it. Depending on how you swing the racket, the ball will move either fast or slow, up or down, and so on. But what about *you*? There are philosophers who believe that you do not differ in any significant way from your racket or the tennis ball: there is someone or something 'swinging' you, making you act the way that you do. It could be God or your DNA, but in either case *you* are not the one *doing* anything. But this is exactly what Aristotle denies. He believes that you are free because you decide to initiate the sequence of events that results in your racket hitting the ball: you see where the ball is headed and decide that it will be in bounds, so you move toward it and swing your arm quickly and precisely, hitting the ball over the net, and, hopefully, winning the point. According to Aristotle's view, we humans occupy a special place in what philosophers call the 'causal series.' Unlike balls and rackets whose movements are entirely determined by prior events and the laws of physics, human beings have the capacity to *initiate* a series of events. It is that ability that constitutes their *freedom*. This is precisely what philosophers mean by metaphysical freedom: humans can initiate actions based on their desires; they are not constrained to act in any particular way, as things like balls and rackets are, although there are certainly constraints on what it is possible for us to do. We humans, initiators of causal sequences, have a distinct way of *being-in-the-world*, to introduce one basic term of Existentialism.

Gradually, with the rise of modern scientific theory, it dawned on philosophers and other thinkers that human beings might not really be free, that our sense of ourselves as having the power to do one thing rather than another might be simply an illusion. Of course, philosophers had already confronted this issue from the beginning of the discipline. For example, Medieval philosophers recognized that God posed a threat to human freedom. If God is omniscient, that is, knows everything, then he also knows what you are going to do before you do it. Even though you *think* you are free, God, using his infinite knowledge, correctly anticipates your actions. But then it sure looks as if your decision is not freely made even though it may feel like it to you, because you could not have done things any differently without contradicting the fact that God has complete foreknowledge. (This idea is raised by the recent film *The Matrix Reloaded* (2003), although there it is not God but 'the Oracle' and 'the Architect' whose 'foreknowledge' threatens human freedom.) Modern science proved to be incredibly successful at explaining and predicting the behavior of all the objects to which it turned its attention. Indeed, as physical theory developed, the universe began to seem like a huge clock that moved, as clocks do, in completely predictable ways that could be understood on the basis of the laws of physics. Could the same be true of *us*? Could we really be just little gears in the great clock of the universe, mere mechanisms in the grand plan of nature?

It's easy for us now to be blasé about the power of science and technology. After all, we're used to the impact that scientific discoveries and technological innovations have had on our lives, even if we are continually being surprised by the latest technological breakthrough that makes our recently purchased iPods or PCs so quickly obsolete. But for people at the beginning of the nineteenth century – when the seeds of Existentialism were being sown – science promised to completely revolutionize human life on the planet. Think about it. Virtually every aspect of how we live our lives is affected by the technological products that modern science and technology provide. The food we eat, the clothes we wear, the sounds we hear, even the sights we see all bear testimony to the ubiquity of the products of technology. And even when we go 'back to nature,' thinking that we are getting away from 'civilization,' technology remains very much in evidence, when, for example, the stream beside which we walk takes the course it does because of the flood control technology that keeps it within its banks.

One consequence of science's great successes was its *hubristic* claim to be able to explain everything. 'Hubris' is Greek for 'overarching pride.' We can illustrate this notion through the well-known story from Greek mythology about Icarus. Icarus was the son of Daedalus, an amazing craftsman. Daedalus fashioned a set of wings for his son out of wax and feathers, and warned him not to fly too close to the sun lest the wax melt, nor too close to the sea lest the feathers get wet. But when Icarus took to the sky, he ignored his father's advice. Intoxicated by flight and thinking himself capable of anything, he soared too close to the sun. Of course, the sun melted his wings, causing him to fall to his death in the sea. Now, modern science can be thought of as having the same sort of hubris as Icarus: intoxicated by its own success, science overreaches itself by maintaining that it can explain everything, even human behavior. But whether science's boast actually is an example of hubris or whether the reach of science truly extends that far remains hotly debated by philosophers to this day.

Let's think about how science might be able to explain the behavior of human beings. Basically, the claim is that science has the capacity to develop an intricate system of laws to explain all human actions. For example, as I sit here in front of my computer, typing this sentence, I think I am making decisions on my own about what to say and how to say it. According to hubristic natural science, however, my perception is false. There are psycho–physical laws about how the human brain works that could, in conjunction with facts about me together with my previous experiences, explain why I just typed the word 'hubristic' or used the story of Daedalus and Icarus as a way to explain the self-conceit of science about the scope of its power.

Science's attempt to explain every feature of the human being was very threatening to many during the nineteenth century, especially as the traditional bases for religious faith became unconvincing to many. The Underground Man is a paradigmatic example of one response to science's claim to see into the depths of our souls. If science could explain everything that a human being does, down to such minutiae as why I chose to type one word rather than another, then my view of myself as a possessor of metaphysical freedom would be merely an illusion. As the Underground Man puts it so well, the human being would be nothing more than a complicated piano key. When I strike the middle-C key on a piano, the key does not have a choice about what it will do: it moves a lever, triggering a hammer to strike a specific string that vibrates at precisely 261.1 cycles per second (hertz), thereby sounding the middle-C. Barring interference, the process is completely inevitable. In contrast, at least since Aristotle people had assured themselves that they were different, for they were the ones who initiated such processes. They were – you guessed it – *free*. But the natural scientists of the early nineteenth century laughed at this idea as merely one more pretense that humans had to learn to shed. After all, these scientists and their predecessors had proved Aristotle wrong about physics and astronomy. As in the account of creation in Genesis, Aristotle thought that the earth was the center of the universe. Yet a succession of great astronomers and physicists – Nicolaus Copernicus, Johannes Kepler, Galileo Galilei, and Sir Isaac Newton – demonstrated that the earth was actually just one planet revolving around the sun. Now we know that the sun is not even the center of the universe. Such discoveries constituted huge threats to the self-image of human beings, a fact attested to by the persecution these first great scientists had to endure because of their theories and the challenge they posed to traditional religious belief. Eventually we got over the threat those theories presented to our sense of ourselves and accepted the cosmological views of the natural scientists. Now all we had to do, according to those working in the very same scientific tradition, was to come to terms with the next threat to our narcissism: our belief that we have a fundamentally different nature from all the other things that exist in the world.

This challenge posed by hubristic natural science and the philosophical schools that supported it was the spark that ignited the philosophical movement of Existentialism. The Underground Man's words convey exactly how this challenge was countered: 'Tell me that I'm no different from a piano key,' we can imagine him to be thinking, 'and I'll do something stupid, unexpected, I might even utter a curse, just to show you that I am different. And if you try to prove to me that nothing I can do undermines your claim that my actions are as completely determined by scientific laws as those of a piano key, I'll even go insane in order not to have to accept your arguments.' In his colorful way, the Underground Man is saying what all the Existentialists believe: nothing, even our ability to think rationally, is more essential to us than our freedom.

Being human

The Underground Man's assertion that he won't accept any proof that he, a human being, is not unique among all the things existing alongside him in the world stakes out the territory that the Existentialists will occupy and develop. Indeed, so distinctive is the human being that, in his renowned book, *Being and Time*, Martin Heidegger (see text box opposite) developed a special word to refer to us: *Dasein*, composed of the two German words for 'there' (*da*) and 'being' (*sein*). Heidegger chose this word for a number of reasons. Characterizing human existence as 'being-there' was his way of asserting the importance of the awareness that we humans have of our own being, that our being has a *there*, exists in a specific place. But he also used this term to make it clear that humans are so distinctive a type of being or existent that they should not be characterized as simply one being among others, the *human* (type of) being. He thought the terminology of the 'Western tradition of metaphysics,' by referring to us as human *beings*, obscured our truly distinctive nature. After all, there are lots of beings in the world. Ants are a type of being and so are tables, chairs, and even rocks. If humans are regarded as just one type of being among others, then it is easy to underestimate their distinctiveness and treat them as more nearly continuous with other types of existents. So calling us *Dasein* was Heidegger's way of emphasizing that we are not just one being among others, but that, on the contrary, there is something completely distinctive about the being of humans.

Martin Heidegger (1889–1976) was one of the most influential philosophers of the twentieth century. His magnum opus, *Being and Time* (1927), played an important role in the formation of Existentialism, sounding many themes that would later become characteristic of the school. Among these are: the distinctive nature of the human being or *Dasein*; the alienation of the human being in its everyday world; others as central to the existence of humans but also as a source of social conformity; authenticity as a distinctive possibility of human existence; and death as the reality a person could focus upon in order to achieve authenticity.

After the publication of *Being and Time*, Heidegger's thinking underwent a profound change and he began to emphasize the importance of human receptivity over activity. Instead of trying to control the conditions of our own existence, Heidegger now asserted, humans should concentrate on noticing the distinctive features of existence itself. As a result, he was critical of contemporary society for its reliance upon technology, which he claimed caused *being* to be obscured.

The most controversial aspect of Heidegger's life was his embracing of Nazism and his service as the Rector (President) of the University of Freiburg under the Nazis. After World War II, he was banned from teaching and was the target of continuing criticism, especially for his failure to explain his support for the Nazis.

Although many are still suspicious of Heidegger's philosophy for its purported fascist tendencies, his writings continue to be extremely influential, particularly for contemporary French thought.

But what exactly about humans makes them such a distinct type of being? To answer this question, we will have to do a bit of metaphysics ourselves. Metaphysics is that branch of philosophy that concerns the nature of existence. Among its tasks is ontology, or enumerating the fundamental types of things that exist. As I have said, it is obvious to everyone that there are many different kinds of beings or entities in the world. What's not so obvious is that each of these has something distinctive about it, something that makes it the specific type of thing that it is. Metaphysicians call this the entity's *nature* or *essence*. Take rocks, for example. What can we say about their nature? Well, for starters, that they are hard and fall if dropped. These features, along with other properties, constitute the nature of a rock, what it is for something to be a rock, its essence. Something that failed to have these features would not be a rock. Now, an analogous claim applies to all things in the world – from dust and dirt to lions and tigers. They all have natures that make them the specific things they are.

According to the Existentialists, humans do not have such a predetermined nature that makes us the distinctive type of thing that we are. Heidegger asserted that what makes *Dasein* unique is that it, alone among existing things, not only lacks a nature in this sense but also *takes its own existence (being) to be an issue for it*. At first glance, this might seem like a peculiar or obscure way to make the point. But with Heidegger, as with all the Existentialists, what initially might seem to be merely an idiosyncratic use of language usually turns out to be a way of registering the result of a great deal of careful reflection upon an important philosophical issue. So, let's see all that Heidegger packed into this unusual formulation about the nature of human beings. First of all, *takes its own existence to be an issue* is Heidegger's way of saying that humans do not just exist – as, say, rocks do – but they are also *aware* of themselves as existing. Unlike those things that simply *are*, we have the capacity to notice *that* we are and *how* we are. Although traditionally this capacity had been conceptualized as our capacity for *self-consciousness*, Heidegger avoided this expression because he believed that thinking in terms of it inevitably led to two of the fundamental questions that Western philosophy never seemed able to answer. These were: whether we could have knowledge of a world external to our own selves (skepticism about external reality), and whether we have an adequate basis for attributing minds to the bodies we see all around us (skepticism about other minds). By avoiding such *dualisms* as *self-and-world* and *mind-and-body*, Heidegger thought Western philosophy could move beyond the insoluble problems that plagued it.

Second, this way of speaking is Heidegger's way of conceptualizing the fundamental freedom we humans have. As he would say, *Dasein* is a being (entity) whose being (way of existing) remains open. Unlike, say, rocks, we are not born having a specific nature, but are free to make our natures. In addition, we are not determined by our past, but always have the option of changing how we act. Even if, for example, you have always been afraid of climbing mountains, you can decide that you are going to go ahead and climb one because you do not want to be a person whose life is determined by her fears. So, in addition to being aware of what we are like, we humans have the capacity to create our own natures through our own free choices. Of course, that very capacity is part of what makes us the distinctive type of being that we are, but this is not, according to the Existentialists, the same as having a determinate nature.

There is an additional reason for Heidegger's usage that it is important to recognize: he wanted to make it clear that human beings are *concerned* about *how* they exist. We are not indifferent to what becomes of us, as, say, rocks are to whether they are part of a mountain or crushed into the gravel that forms the path leading to our front door. To help us understand this idea, it is useful to return to *Hamlet*. Heidegger would say that Hamlet's case clearly illustrates this aspect of *Dasein*'s being, for Hamlet is deeply concerned about *how* he will be, specifically, whether he will avenge his father's death, as a dutiful son would, or fail to and act like, as he puts it, a 'rogue and peasant slave.' How he chooses to be, what he chooses to do, is not a matter about which Hamlet is indifferent, nor is there anyone else who can make Hamlet's decision for him. In the end, it is completely up to him, the single, existing individual, Hamlet. In sum, then, Heidegger views *Dasein* as a being that is free, aware, and concerned.

Consciousness

The philosopher Jean-Paul Sartre (see text box opposite) is 'the Existentialist par excellence.' Sartre was deeply influenced by Heidegger, whose ideas he encountered while a student in Germany between the two World Wars. However, Sartre developed his own, unique way of thinking about the freedom that we humans have. Even though he seems to agree that the term 'human *being*' is not an appropriate way to characterize us, Sartre uses a different term to refer to human beings: *la réalité humaine* or human reality. This apparently minor terminological shift allows Sartre to develop a different set of theoretical concepts for understanding human existence.

In 1929, Sartre formed a life-long liaison with the young French philosopher, Simone de Beauvoir, and they were very public about the nature of their commitment: Although their relationship was the primary one in their lives, they agreed to allow each other the freedom to pursue other romantic affairs, so as not to unduly limit each other's freedom. Their open acknowledgment of this unusual agreement caused an international furor and helped to propel Sartre and de Beauvoir onto the world stage.

Jean-Paul Sartre (1905–1980) is probably the most well known of the Existentialists, having attained great fame because of his writings, his life-style, and his political activism. Sartre was a prolific writer whose writings spanned a wide range of genres. His philosophical works include two major treatises, *Being and Nothingness* (1943) and *Critique of Dialectical Reason* (1960). However, Sartre was more famous for his plays – *The Flies* (1943) and *No Exit* (1944), for example – and novels – like *Nausea* (1938), perhaps the greatest philosophical novel ever written. In addition to works in these genres, Sartre also published an autobiography, *The Words* (1964), and works of literary biography such as *Saint Genet* (1952), a biographical study of the French writer Jean Genet, and *The Family Idiot* (1971–1972), a study of the French novelist, Gustave Flaubert.

Sartre was the model of the engaged intellectual. During World War II, he was active in the underground for a time. After the war, together with de Beauvoir and the Existentialist philosopher Maurice Merleau-Ponty, he founded the journal *Les Temps Modernes*, in which many articles on the topics of the day were published. Sartre was honored with the Nobel Prize for Literature but he refused it lest it seem that he endorsed its bourgeois values. He continued his political interventions until his death.

Like Heidegger, Sartre believed that human beings have a distinctive manner of existing. In order to acknowledge this, he attempted to characterize the different ontological features of this unique being by investigating the nature of 'consciousness.' Ever since René Descartes founded modern Western philosophy at the beginning of the seventeenth century, human beings were conceptualized within that tradition as possessing *consciousness*, that is, as having minds with which they perceive the world and reflect upon it. Sartre accepted this basic idea, but gave it his own, unique spin.

Sartre began by contrasting the being of consciousness with the being of all other things. Employing the terminology of traditional philosophical metaphysics, he characterized the being of all non-human entities as *existence in-itself* (*en-soi*). This entailed, he claimed, that any particular thing is exactly what it is. While this seems completely obvious, we will see that the idea acquires added significance once it is contrasted with the type of being that consciousness has. Here, it is sufficient to note that Sartre thinks everything that is not a consciousness has a nature that it must embody to be the thing that it is. This is only the beginning of Sartre's analysis, however.

One might consider this assertion as Sartre clearing his throat before he makes his next startling claim: Consciousness is unique among existing entities in that it exists *for-itself* (*pour-soi*). But what does it mean for something to exist for-itself? Something exists for-itself if it has an idea of itself. This idea of itself must be something that consciousness is aware of, and, therefore, forms the content of its thinking. For example, consider Antoine Roquentin, the main character of Sartre's philosophical novel, *Nausea*. At one point in the novel, he is sitting in a park in Paris, looking at the root of a tree. The first element of his consciousness is simply his perception of the tree. Sartre terms this aspect of Roquentin's experience his *positional* consciousness. But Roquentin doesn't just perceive the tree, he is also aware, or so Sartre claims, that he is perceiving a tree and, thus, has a *nonpositional* consciousness of himself. This means that human beings are, in this specific sense, split or bifurcated beings: a person does not, as a consciousness, simply perceive the world; she simultaneously is aware of herself perceiving the world. Consciousness is the only entity in the world that does not just exist, but also presents itself to itself as existing.

There is more to the idea of existence for-itself, however, than the fact that I am aware at each moment of the way I am existing. Take the fact that I am now the author of a book about Existentialism. This is not something that *had* to be true of me. For many years, I had entertained the thought of writing a book like this one, but decided against it, prioritizing other projects in its place. Although I ultimately decided to write the book, I did not have to: there was nothing in my nature as a human being that forced me to write it. Another example: seeing chocolate cake on a menu does not force me to eat it, though I love chocolate and could eat the cake if I decided to. Chocoholics, beware! Existentialists will not accept your addiction to chocolate as an excuse: you could have refrained from eating that delicious piece of chocolate cake if you had chosen to. Why? Because, as Sartre would put it, there was *nothing* in your nature as a consciousness that required you to be a 'cake-eater.' You were free to eat the cake but didn't have to. What both these examples show is that human beings are not necessitated to *be* anything.

In this respect, a being *for-itself* is different from a being *in-itself*. Rocks have to fall: they have no choice in the matter. In contrast, beings for-themselves must make choices, but the outcome of those choices is not determined by anything. As consciousnesses, we do not have to be authors of books on Existentialism or cake-eaters. In fact, we do not have to be any specific thing at all. This is because, to cite Sartre again, as a for-itself consciousness is a *nothing*.

Now being told that you are a 'nothing' probably does not strike you as a piece of good news. After all, there are probably lots of 'things' that you are and are proud of being. Maybe you are a good athlete or a good student, a good singer or a good writer, a good mother or a good daughter. When Sartre says that you, as a consciousness, are a nothing, should you take it as an insult?

Actually, it is the highest compliment that Sartre could pay you, for he is telling you that you are free. Because you are a nothing, you are free to do whatever you want to. The situation is different – let us leave rocks aside for the moment – with animals. A dog cannot choose to chase a squirrel or not. Animals have instincts that determine their behavior. Dogs don't decide,

'Hey, I think I'll bark at that squirrel and drag my owner down the sidewalk as I try to capture it.' They just do it, propelled by their instincts: 'Squirrel at 45 degrees? Pursue!' But we are not like that. There is nothing that we have to do, no course of action that we have to follow. Even if I have amazing skills at playing the piano, I do not have to play one. Just because the sight of that key lime pie causes my mouth to water, I do not have to consume it ... unlike my dog, Amber, who makes a beeline for any piece of food that falls to the floor without, as we say, a second thought. Although I could explain my action by saying that I am full or on a diet or would just prefer something else today, I could also refuse to explain it. To use some more of Sartre's difficult terminology, as a conscious being I can *nihilate* the desire to eat the pie. That is, I can control it and send it packing, so to speak. After all, this is what it is to be a free being.

There is a song that Groucho sings in the Marx Brothers' 1932 film *Horse Feathers*. He plays a college president who sings this refrain in the film's opening number:

> I don't know what they have to say
> It makes no difference anyway;
> Whatever it is, I'm against it!

This ditty can function as a comic rendering of Sartre's theory of the nature of consciousness: Although we don't *have* to nihilate every desire we find ourselves having – as we do when we think, 'I'm hungry but I'm on a diet so I won't eat' or 'I have a test I should be studying for but it's Saturday night, so I won't bother' – we have the ability to do so. This is the metaphysical fact about us as human beings – 'consciousnesses' in Sartre's terminology – that grounds the Existentialist view of freedom as the most basic feature of the human being.

Sartre's use of terms such as 'nothing,' 'nihilation,' and 'nothingness' can be very confusing, but to fully understand his view of consciousness, we must submerge ourselves a bit deeper in these muddy waters. Let's begin our unpacking of this difficult terminology by following Sartre himself and think about a situation in which something does not work as we expect it to. Sartre's example is a car that has broken down (*Being and Nothingness*, 38f.). A mechanic, when confronted with such a car, inspects its various parts: the carburetor, the spark plugs, and so on. But what is he doing, specifically, when he looks at, say, the carburetor? Sartre unhelpfully makes the following statement: 'If I question the carburetor, it is because I consider it possible that "there is nothing there" in the carburetor.' We can make some progress in grasping what Sartre is getting at if we ask what the mechanic is *looking for*. The carburetor is quite obviously there, so he cannot be looking for *it*. Indeed, he cannot be looking, in a puzzled sort of way, for any thing that is there, since everything he can possibly see is already there and visible. No, the mechanic must be looking for something that is not there or, as Sartre would have it, the *nothing* that *is* there. In order to be able to see why the car is not working as it should, we have to 'inject' into the world of existing things a *non-being*, the functioning car, which is not actually present. And this non-being, this *nothing*, is something that is present in the world only because we human beings place it there. It is thus a basic feature of being human, according to Sartre, to be in contact with *nothingness*, for only in this way can we make determinations about how things might have been otherwise.

This is a very important aspect of Sartre's theory, for he has just claimed that *consciousness* contributes *nothingness* to *being*. Given that his magnum opus is entitled *Being and Nothingness*, we really need to understand this aspect of his metaphysics. Sartre makes another attempt to clarify this murky notion in the context of a café. (Many of Sartre's examples involve cafés, since he spent so much time contemplating and writing in them.) In this case, he considers what must be true for him to notice that Pierre, who is supposed to meet him in the café, is not there.

First of all, Sartre notes that the café is completely full of beings: there are no 'ontological gaps' in it. Yet, in a sense this makes it difficult to understand how we can notice Pierre not being there, for there is no 'absence' present in the café of which we can be aware. It is not as if Pierre is there in a ghostly form that enables us to notice his actual absence. What is required, Sartre tells us in a stunning phenomenological analysis (see text box opposite), is that we *nihilate* or negate the presence of everyone and everything in the room, so they can form a background to our noticing Pierre's absence. It is as if we scan the room and, for every item that is present, quickly say, 'No!' thereby 'negating' it as an indication of his presence or absence.

But, after we have thus prepared the field for noticing Pierre's absence, we still have not done all that is necessary to become aware of it. There still seems to be nothing for us to be conscious of when we notice Pierre's absence. Sartre solves this problem by claiming that we make a *second* nihilation, this time in regard to Pierre himself. We become aware of Pierre in the mode of negation, as a *nothing*. But this *nothing* – a *nothingness* that lies at the heart of being, Sartre tells us in his picturesque language – is something that we human beings have added to the world. Without us, there would be *no nothingness there*, so to speak. As human beings, we make a distinctive contribution to the structure of being, of existence: we contribute nothingness to being.

But how does Sartre's analysis of the human as a nihilating being amount to an acknowledgment of our freedom, which was, after all, the point of my introducing it? Sartre's claim is that only a being that is *itself* a nothingness can be aware of nothingness itself:

> The being by which nothingness arrives in the world must nihilate nothingness in its being, and even so it still runs the risk of establishing nothingness as a transcendent in the very heart of immanence unless it nihilates nothingness in its being *in connection with its own being*. (*Being and Nothingness*, 57)

Phenomenology is a method of philosophical analysis that was first articulated in a systematic fashion by the philosopher Edmund Husserl (1859–1938) and later adopted by almost all the subsequent Existentialist thinkers, including Martin Heidegger and Jean-Paul Sartre. Although it has come in for a great deal of criticism, especially from the post-modernists, it remains an important philosophical method that is still widely practiced among Continental philosophers.

The focus of the phenomenological method is on the experience of conscious human beings. What it attempts to do, by means of a precise and exact description of various different types of experience, is to lay bare the actual structures such experiences have. It claims that a phenomenological analysis results in our gaining access to the correct nature of the concepts or ideas so analyzed. For example, many philosophers were impressed by the concept of time as it was used within natural science and they took this concept to be our natural concept of time. But Husserl presented a phenomenological account of time in which he attempted to capture the experience of a temporal being like ourselves. Using concepts such as 'running off' – which attempts to specify how the present inevitably anticipates its own demise into the past – Husserl presented a conception of time that was much closer to our ordinary experience of it, and he argued that this was the basic notion of time from which the scientific one could be derived.

In general, phenomenologists attempt to account for all the different 'phenomena' that structure our world, from time and space to objects and other people. In so doing, they hope to put philosophy on a more secure ('scientific') footing than it previously had.

This is one of those sentences that makes students drop their philosophy classes and professional philosophers study David Hume instead of Sartre. Still, the point is an important one that we cannot pass over. Sartre is asserting that consciousness, the being that is aware of nothingness, must itself be a nothingness in order to have that awareness. We do not have to worry about whether Sartre puts forth a good argument to establish this claim, but only focus on its meaning: consciousness is itself a nothingness, as well as the being that injects nothingness into being. And this is intended to be good news, for it is Sartre's explanation of our inherent freedom as humans.

The example of Pierre's absence focused on a rather singular case of our ability to nihilate another person's presence. A more central case of nihilation, at least from the point of view of explaining our freedom, involves us taking own self as the content of our consciousness. So, let's assume that I have always wanted to own a Ferrari. I think to myself the true thought, 'Tom wants a Ferrari.' Does this mean that I have to try to find a way to become a Ferrari owner? We all would agree, I think, that the answer is, 'No.' I could decide that, given the price of gas, say, it just does not make financial sense for me to own and drive a Ferrari. Or my social conscience might get the better of me and help me decide that, much as I would like to own a Ferrari, it would not be good for the future of the planet for me to drive such a gas guzzler. Or I might simply decide that a Ferrari is not the car I really want, for a Maserati is so much more stylish. But in any of these cases, I would have to entertain the thought, 'Tom is a Ferrari owner,' in the mode of negation. That is, as a human being I am able to nihilate any content that I can entertain in my consciousness. But this means that I do not have to think or be any specific thing, that I am, as a nihilating being, free to think or be whatever I want.

Being what one is not

As we have seen, Sartre claimed that everything which exists other than consciousness is what it is. So far, so good. But only the human being, he adds, *is what it is not* and *is not what it is*. Once again, we find Sartre using deliberately paradoxical language to express his philosophical insight. This means we'll have to do a bit of work to understand it.

Unfortunately, the best way to do so is to consider another pair of puzzling terms: *transcendence* and *facticity*. Human beings, because they are free, exhibit what Sartre calls 'transcendence,' an ability to move beyond their given circumstances. Our freely chosen *projects* – another favorite Sartrean term – are evidence of our transcendence, for we take it upon ourselves to create something through our own actions. Nonetheless, in engaging in our 'projects' – a term used to refer to any of the undertakings we choose – we work in a given context. Unlike traditional views of God, we don't create *ex nihilo* (out of nothing). We exist within a context that includes facts about both ourselves and the world. This is what Sartre calls 'facticity.' Human beings are, as he says, factical as well as transcendent beings. What this means is that we are able to undertake our projects, in which we seek to go beyond the given conditions in which we find ourselves, only in those very conditions themselves. Our transcendence requires facticity as its necessary correlate.

We are now ready to take up Sartre's puzzling claim that a human is the only entity in the world that 'is what it is not and is not what it is.' Our previous discussion allows us to understand what Sartre means. First, we are not – as transcending beings – what we are – factically – for we can change and make of ourselves something different from what we appear to be at any time; and, second, we are also – once again as transcending beings – what we are not – factically – for our projects often involve creating ourselves to be in the future something that we are not now.

It might be helpful here to think of the Post-Impressionist painter, Paul Gauguin. In 1884, Gauguin was a stockbroker living in Copenhagen with a wife and two children. The next year, he decided that, in his present life, he was not able to be who he was, so he abandoned his family and his career to devote himself exclusively to painting. Eventually, he wound up in Tahiti and created his own unique style of painting. Gauguin's life is a clear example of a person who was not, in his bourgeois life, who he really was. His decision to risk everything to become who he was is a good example of Sartre's notion that we are factical beings with the possibility of transcendence.

Sartre had a tendency to turn profound insights into slogans. In the essay 'Existentialism is a Humanism,' Sartre characterized the human lack of a preordained nature this way: 'Man's existence precedes his essence.' As a slogan, this is pretty nice. It suggests that humans come into existence – are born – without any nature or essence to them. The birth of a child begins a process in which a being whose nature is undetermined, whose future is open, comes into existence. Only in the course of living will that child determine exactly what kind of being it is. Its being, to revert to another abstract philosophical term, is *becoming*. In making the myriad decisions one must over the course of a life – Will I study the piano? Should I go out for the basketball team? Do I really like Millie? – a child transforms herself from a nothingness into a determinate being, a person with a specific character. She might become a scientist or an artist. She might have a trustworthy character or be totally unreliable. Ultimately, her *essence* comes to be as a result of her living her life.

So, in one sense, Sartre's slogan does a nice job of capturing the nature of human life: Our 'essence' is to *become* what we are. Unfortunately, there are some deep problems with this idea that make it difficult to endorse as an adequate way to conceptualize our freedom. After all, even if we are free, there is much about us that is determined for us. Take one simple fact: how tall we are. This is something we cannot change. Is it an essential part of me that I am 5′ 9″ tall? Most likely not, for I would, *in essence*, be the same person I am even if I were an inch shorter or taller. Sartre needs to further explain how such features do not contradict his claim that existence precedes essence.

Although he does not discuss it in 'Existentialism is a Humanism,' Sartre does address this potential contradiction by asserting that humans do not exist in a vacuum but always in a specific *situation*, that we are factical as well as transcending beings. Although we are free, we exercise our freedom within concrete situations. In fact, only in the context of a specific situation does our exercise of freedom make sense. When I am presented with a choice that is not of my own making, one that is a result of my situation, I get to exercise my freedom and to show that I am a being who exists through my own nihilation of my circumstances. For only in such cases can I exercise my freedom by nihilating a given content.

So, for Sartre, human beings, so long as they are alive, are never a finished product. Existing in a specific, factical situation, we have to exercise our freedom to decide how to transcend it. And as we act, we create ourselves *post facto* or after the fact. But although we do create ourselves in the course of our lives, we are never what we have made of ourselves, for that created self becomes simply another factor in our factical situation. And, as transcendent beings, we are once again free to become what we are not. This is an idea whose implications we will explore in the next chapter.

Common to both Sartre and Heidegger, then, is their recognition that the human being is a unique entity in the world in virtue of its freedom. Although they conceptualize this freedom in different ways, they each accept the Existentialist belief that human beings are a unique type of existent. Their emphasis on human freedom as something that is essential to our natures, making us the distinctive type of entity that we are, is the first crucial theme developed by the Existentialists.

But to simply assert that the Existentialists take freedom to be a defining characteristic of humans is to miss the radicality of their view, for other philosophers – Kant, for example – would agree that freedom is a central characteristic of the human being.

A first thing that is distinctive about the Existentialists' account is their taking our freedom as human beings to entail that each of us has a fundamental and ongoing concern with the nature of our own existence, of how we are and will be. By claiming that we each have this abiding concern with who we are and what we might become, the Existentialists give a unique spin to the notion that our freedom is what distinguishes us from other beings.

But, important as this idea is, it only begins the Existentialist analysis of human freedom. In the next chapter, we will look at a second aspect of human freedom emphasized by the Existentialists: that we are, as Sartre put it, *condemned* to be free. Even though the Existentialists believe that freedom is the most important thing about us, they recognize that freedom is not an unalloyed benefit to us. From their point of view, analyzing this fact provides a necessary corrective to the philosophical tradition's celebration of freedom and marks a distinctive attitude developed by this unique school of philosophical thinking.

2

Freedom

In the last chapter, we explored the Existentialists' contention that freedom is an essential feature of human life. Yet, as I remarked, this view marks only the first stage of the Existentialists' analysis. The Existentialists also hold freedom to be something from which human beings recoil. But at first sight, this claim appears quite strange, indeed, nearly paradoxical. After all, most people think that freedom is a good thing. And the aspiration for freedom has inspired many people to improve the circumstances in which they live. How, then, could freedom be something from which we turn away, as if it were something deserving our fear?

To understand this aspect of the Existentialists' account of human freedom, we are going to turn our attention, once again, to a literary work of Fyodor Dostoevsky. This time, we will be looking at one of the greatest creations in all of Western literature: Dostoevsky's parable of the Grand Inquisitor, a chapter from his masterpiece, *The Brothers Karamazov* (1880). The plot of Dostoevsky's novel revolves around the patricide of Fyodor Karamazov. There is a great deal more to the novel than that, however, for it includes, among other things, a number of discussions among the Karamazov brothers about the grounds for religious faith and ethical behavior. It is in this context that we find the great parable of the Grand Inquisitor.

Ivan, the middle brother, has serious doubts about religion. As part of a conversation he has with his younger brother, Alyosha, who is studying to become a priest, he narrates the parable. The story involves Jesus' return to Earth during the Spanish Inquisition at the end of the fifteenth century. The

Medieval Catholic Church employed the Inquisition to root out impieties of all sorts, especially the presence of false converts to Catholicism who continued to practice their own religions. The Grand Inquisitor was the Church official who decided exactly how the Inquisition would carry out its mission.

In the parable, Jesus has arrived in Seville upon his return to Earth. When the Inquisition discovers him there, the Grand Inquisitor has him apprehended and imprisoned. The parable consists mostly of the speech that the Grand Inquisitor makes to Jesus to explain why he has arrested him and will, if necessary, have him killed once more.

The idea that someone would decide to kill Jesus for a second time is both shocking and provocative. After all, Christians think of Jesus' crucifixion as the greatest tragedy in world history: our actually killing the son of God. The parable becomes even more outrageous when we realize that his persecutor, the Grand Inquisitor, is himself a Christian – rather than a harsh pagan ruler – who readily acknowledges Jesus' divinity. What could possibly motivate a religious man like the Grand Inquisitor to commit the monstrous sin of killing the son of God, and for the second time in human history?

The Grand Inquisitor gives a chilling answer to this question that explains his intentions. Using virtually the same language to justify *his* actions that Jesus had used to justify *his*, according to the gospels, the Grand Inquisitor tells Jesus that it is his love for humankind that has motivated his crimes: that *he*, not Jesus, is the one who has truly taken the sins of human beings upon himself. But this seems preposterous. How could the Inquisitor see himself as loving human beings more than someone who gave his very life for them?

The answer is that the Inquisitor believes that, although Jesus' motivation was good, he made a very serious mistake: overestimating human beings. Jesus did this, according to the Inquisitor, by believing that humans valued freedom more than their own physical and psychological well-being. The Inquisitor, on the other hand, is clear that most human beings prefer their own happiness. As a result, the Inquisitor has had to work hard to correct the mistakes Jesus had made. Out of *his* love for humankind, the Inquisitor has spared human beings the anguish inherent in being free by using his earthly power to keep them well fed and entertained: hence, bread and miracles.

Addressing Jesus as a prosecutor would, the Inquisitor cites evidence to prove how badly Jesus misunderstood people. Central to his case is Jesus' response to his temptation by the devil. According to the gospels, the devil presented Jesus with three temptations in the desert. The first was to make bread out of stone to satisfy his hunger, to which Jesus replied that man does not live by bread alone; then, when the devil suggested to Jesus that he jump from a pinnacle and be saved by angels in order to show that he was the son of God, Jesus responded that the devil should not tempt the Lord; the third and final temptation was the offer of earthly power in exchange for Jesus worshiping the devil, to which Jesus rejoined that only God was to be worshiped. In essence, Jesus rejected *food*, *miracles*, and *earthly power* as sources for people's faith in God. Instead, he asked people to believe in God of their own free will, and it is precisely for this that the Inquisitor rebukes him:

> You want to go into the world, and you are going empty-handed, with some promise of freedom, which they in their simplicity and innate lawlessness cannot even comprehend, which they dread and fear – for nothing has ever been more insufferable for man and for human society than freedom! (*Brothers Karamazov*, 252)

The Inquisitor's point is that the devil understood human beings better than Jesus did: people do not want their freedom; it only scares and troubles them. Instead, what people really desire is happiness, that is, temporal rather than otherworldly satisfaction.

Yet this is exactly what Jesus refused to give them. Food, miracles, and authority provide humans with happiness by giving them full bellies and minds too busy with entertaining spectacles to think about troubling issues.

Thus, the Inquisitor has taken upon himself the task of completing Jesus' mission, something he intends to accomplish by employing all the means that Jesus had rejected as not suitable as vehicles for inspiring faith in human beings. Once again sounding very much like Jesus himself, he explains that the Inquisition – and by this he means the entire apparatus of the Catholic Church – has taken upon itself Jesus' own program of assuming the sins of human beings:

> We will tell them that every sin will be redeemed if it is committed with our permission; and that we allow them to sin because we love them, and as for the punishment for these sins, very well, we take it upon ourselves. And we will take it upon ourselves, and they will adore us as benefactors, who have borne their sins before God. (*Brothers Karamazov*, 259)

Unlike Jesus, the Church leaders take the sins of humankind upon themselves rather cynically, because they do not believe in 'sin' any more than they believe in the necessity of Divine 'punishment.' They know that the rules they promulgate – in which talk of sin and punishment is prominent – are white lies, whose aim is nothing but the alleviation of the suffering of human beings. The Church has taken, we are to understand, the freedom of the masses away from them in order to bestow upon them the blessing of happiness. From the Inquisitor's point of view, freedom and happiness are antithetical values, and when faced with a choice between them, it is clear that most human beings prefer happiness. So the Inquisitor and his minions have chosen to suffer in order to allow others contentment. He concludes by telling Jesus: 'And everyone will be happy, all the millions of creatures, except for the hundred thousand of those who govern them. For only we, we who keep the mystery, only we shall be unhappy' (*Brothers Karamazov*, 259).

As we look back over the events of the twentieth century, we cannot help but be struck by the brutality and barbarism that so frequently swept over disparate regions of the globe. The parable of the Grand Inquisitor offers a unique perspective to help us understand what transpired. For Dostoevsky realized that it does not take evil people to perpetrate atrocities. In fact, the Grand Inquisitor is not a terrible person in Dostoevsky's view. He truly is motivated by a deep love for humanity. Yet he does terrible things, as symbolized by his willingness to sacrifice Jesus to the Inquisition's mission. Dostoevsky explains this puzzle by asserting that people perpetrate social evil not because they have evil aims, but because they think they are better than other people and know what is best for them. Their faith in their own mission allows them to do evil because they believe they have unique access to 'the truth.' As a result, they believe that people who do not comprehend their 'truth' need to be guided by themselves and others who are 'in the know.' Thus, a small group of knowledgeable insiders can embrace all sorts of ill-treatment of outsiders.

The prescient and transgressive nature of Dostoevsky's parable may seem unique, but similar ideas about the human preference for happiness over freedom animate a variety of contemporary works of art. Consider, for example, the Wachowski Brothers' film, *The Matrix* (1999). In the film, human beings are held captive by a network of computers that harnesses the humans' neurological processes for energy. To get humans to accept their lot, the network feeds directly into their brains an illusory world that resembles our everyday reality. The film's plot revolves around a small group of free rebels who try to liberate their captive brethren. However, one of the rebels, Cypher (Joe Pantoliano), is a turncoat who sells out his comrades in order to return to the fictive world manipulated by the computers rather than accept the harsh conditions of 'reality.' He explains his choice by saying, 'I know this steak doesn't exist. I know that when I put it in my mouth, the Matrix is telling my brain that it is juicy and delicious. After nine years, you know what I realize? Ignorance is bliss.' In saying that he prefers the illusions generated by the Matrix, Cypher is echoing the claims made by the Grand Inquisitor about people in general: they prefer happiness to freedom. Even though Cypher is aware that his choice to go back into the Matrix means that he will be living in an illusory world, he prefers that life of imaginary satisfaction to the inconveniences and difficulties inherent in the life of a free person. His choice provides, in effect, the direct testimony of one of the Grand Inquisitor's subjects: when given a clear choice between a difficult life predicated on truth and freedom and an easy one based on illusion and satisfaction, he unhesitatingly chooses that of illusion and satisfaction.

Dostoevsky himself was a faithful Christian. He wrote the parable of the Grand Inquisitor in order to illustrate what is wrong with an institution like the Catholic Church: it contradicts the real sources of religious belief. Most readers, however, are more convinced by the Inquisitor's reasoning than they are by Dostoevsky's attempt to refute it, for it embodies an important truth about human beings: freedom is, at best, something about which we are ambivalent.

'The Grand Inquisitor,' then, is an argument for the contention that freedom is not the most important value that human beings hold. But the argument of Dostoevsky's great work still does not show that we are *ambivalent* about freedom, only that there are other things that are more important to us, like physical well-being and emotional contentment. How, then, do the Existentialists make the case for the stronger claim that freedom is something most people *fear*?

Fearing freedom

We can get some help here by recalling the troubles that Hamlet had with behaving in the manner he thought he should. The apparently simple fact that any action he took could not be undone made Hamlet hesitate, and that hesitation had fatal consequences for both himself and others. At one point, Hamlet himself recognizes that he has been hesitating too long, blaming 'some craven scruple/Of thinking too precisely on the event.' Yet, even though he resolves, 'O, from this time forth,/My thoughts be bloody, or be nothing worth,' he continues to vacillate and procrastinate (*Hamlet* III, viii, 40–1 and 65–6).

From the Existentialist point of view, Hamlet's crisis reflects the fundamental metaphysical fact about human beings we have been exploring: that the much-vaunted freedom we possess is actually a source of much of our trouble and pain. In fact, according to the Existentialists, most people react so negatively to the deleterious effects that freedom leaves in its wake that they would prefer to live a life without the pain resulting from possessing it. According to the Existentialists, the following is the motto most people live by: it is better to be a pig satisfied than a human being dissatisfied; better to be a satisfied fool than Socrates, troubled but free. (This is an inversion of John Stuart Mill's actual slogan, expounded during his explanation of the ethical theory of Utilitarianism: 'It is better to be a human being dissatisfied than a pig satisfied; better to be Socrates dissatisfied than a fool satisfied.')

Once again, Sartre provides the philosophical articulation of this point of view with a clear and cogent explanation of why we humans fear our own freedom: it brings responsibility in its wake and it's that that daunts us. Sartre points out that a free person has to accept complete responsibility for the choices he or she makes. This is a consequence of our 'abandonment,' the fact that there are no gods who determine how we shall act. In Sartre's retelling of Aeschylus' *Orestia* in his play *The Flies*, Orestes clearly asserts that his essence lies in his own freedom:

> ORESTES [to Zeus]: You are the king of gods, king of stones and stars, king of the waves of the sea. But you are not the king of man.
>
> ZEUS: Impudent spawn! So I am not your king? Who, then, made you?
>
> ORESTES: You. But you blundered; you should not have made me free.
>
> ZEUS: I gave you freedom so that you might serve me.
>
> ORESTES: Perhaps. But now it has turned against its giver. And neither you nor I can undo what has been done.
>
> ZEUS: Ah, at last! So this is your excuse?
>
> ORESTES: I am not excusing myself.
>
> ZEUS: No? Let me tell you it sounds much like an excuse, this freedom whose slave you claim to be.
>
> ORESTES: Neither slave nor master. I *am* my freedom. No sooner had you created me than I ceased to be yours. (*The Flies*, III, 120–1)

Zeus clearly believes that Orestes ought to act as Zeus wishes him to. In the context of Greek culture, after all, Zeus created all humans, including Orestes. But Orestes just as surely asserts his own independence from Zeus, claiming that Zeus's gift of freedom has resulted in Orestes being able to act according to his own lights, without any regard for the desires of his creator.

This gives an unexpected spin to the notion of abandonment, for in *The Flies* it is clearly Orestes who abandons Zeus and not, as we might expect, the other way around. On this interesting interpretation of our situation as humans, it is we who have abandoned the gods by no longer giving them control over our actions. But if we accept this point of view, it is hard to maintain Orestes' air of bold defiance. After all, there is a great deal of security to be had from seeing oneself as simply following someone else's orders, as Zeus tells Orestes he should. When one does so, one does not need to feel responsibility for what one has done. A knife, for example, is not responsible for cutting someone; it is the person who wields it who bears the responsibility. Similarly, if we were truly just Zeus's minions, it would be he – and not we – who would be responsible for our actions.

But in the face of our abandonment of the gods, it is we who are responsible for our actions. What's frightening about this is that we have to bear this responsibility completely on our own. If we do something worthwhile, then that fact is one that does not scare us; but if we do something shameful or destructive, then we have no one to blame but ourselves. And this is a circumstance that most of us find, at least some of the time, completely overwhelming.

Think back, once again, to Hamlet's situation. In a Sartrean view, what terrifies Hamlet and makes him hesitant to take his revenge, is simply that he has to accept responsibility for his action. What if he is wrong about what Claudius has done? Then he would sin by killing Claudius. Hamlet realizes the weight of his responsibility for his actions. As a result, he continues to question himself. He wonders whether he has enough evidence to act and, thinking that he does not, decides to get more rather than to act precipitously. Recognizing that his own self-consciousness makes him reflect obsessively about the consequences of his actions, Hamlet explains that his fear of taking responsibility for his actions has caused him to delay taking the necessary step: 'Thus conscience [i.e., consciousness] does make cowards of us all' (III, iii, 83). Although Hamlet blames his self-consciousness, Sartre would claim that what it is at the root of his tragedy is his clear acknowledgment of his freedom, abandonment, and responsibility. In light of these three factors, it is amazing that we ever feel ourselves ready to take bold and decisive actions.

There are a number of further reasons why our awareness of our freedom shakes us to the core. Consider, for example, the fact that there are many ways in which we do not have complete control of the outcome of our actions. For instance, whenever we act, we do so on the basis of a vast range of expectations about the course of events in the world that we take for granted. When I wrote this sentence, for example, I assumed that no new use of the words I write will suddenly come into being and cause you to misunderstand what I wanted to say. This assumption does not always hold true. Think of the change that has occurred in the meaning of the word 'gay.' When I was growing up in the 1950s and 1960s, its primary meaning was happy or light-hearted; now, of course, it refers primarily to homosexuality. As a result, many song lyrics and titles from prior generations with the word 'gay' in them now have a meaning their authors did not intend. Cole Porter, for example, cannot be credited with prescience for the title of his 1932 musical, *A Gay Divorce*.

Although this example is relatively trivial, the differences between our assumptions about how the world is and the nature of reality itself can give rise to tragic consequences. In Sartre's story 'The Wall,' a prisoner during the Spanish Civil War faces death unless he reveals the whereabouts of a fellow freedom fighter. The prisoner gives his captors what he thinks is false information about the whereabouts of his comrade. When it turns out that his comrade has, unknown to the prisoner, actually gone to the location he has revealed, the prisoner is freed as a result of having betrayed him. For Sartre, this story illustrates, in addition to the horrors of war, how our actions can have consequences that we neither foresee nor intend. The reason that this is a terrifying prospect for us, according to Sartre, is that we are responsible for the consequences of our actions, even those that we do not intend. So the prisoner who unintentionally betrays his comrade is, despite his good intentions, a traitor to his cause. Actions and their effects matter, not one's intentions, as far as Sartre is concerned.

This is a tough-minded view, one that counters much of our ordinary moral understanding of ourselves. One of the important consequences of the Protestant Reformation for Western culture was a growing emphasis on intentions rather than actions. The Catholic Church had stressed the importance of rituals as markers of religious belief, as in the Mass. In its focus on an individual's private relationship to God, Protestantism saw the interior lives of people as more significant than their external behavior. Moreover, the standard views of people in the twenty-first century remain significantly influenced by this revolution. Think of such common sayings as 'It's not whether you win or lose but how you play the game.' One way of understanding this adage – often seen as laughable in these days of seemingly unbridled competition – is as claiming that what matters are not external factors which are not completely within one's control, but the internal attitudes one takes to one's actions, which are.

Bad Faith

Although this reassessment of the source of value in human life initiated by the Protestant Reformation was in many ways a progressive one, the Existentialists see it as having serious negative consequences for human beings. In particular, Existentialists believe that an emphasis on intentions rather than actions encourages the tendency human beings have to deceive themselves about why they do what they do. Sartre calls such self-deception 'Bad Faith.' This concept is central to the ethical perspective that Sartre develops, for any action that exhibits Bad Faith is liable to moral criticism.

In his famous play *No Exit*, Sartre provides a clear illustration of this form of self-deception. The play takes place in hell, even though Sartre, as an atheist, did not think that hell really exists. Unlike traditional visions of hell as a fiery place where physical torture of the guilty occurs, Sartre imagines it as a simply furnished room with no mirrors and an unlocked door. In this unusual setting, three characters must live together for eternity: Garcin, a newspaper reporter who worries that people think him a coward; Estelle, a beautiful young woman who killed the baby she had with her lover in order not to alienate her rich husband; and Inez, a lesbian who seduced away from her husband a woman who eventually killed both Inez and herself. Each of these characters suffers from an inability to acknowledge these important facts about him- or herself; each thinks that he or she has a 'real' character that is different from – and superior to – the character one would attribute to him or her on the basis of his or her actions. Garcin, for example, denies that he is a coward, saying that he has lacked the right occasion to prove his bravery. Of course, Garcin is deceiving himself, for he failed to act like a hero at a crucial moment in his life when he was presented with the opportunity to do so. His attempt at an excuse is simply an instance of Bad Faith, according to Sartre, a failure to acknowledge that he is precisely the person who his actions show him to be: a coward.

We will return to Sartre's play later, in the context of the role that others have in our lives. Here, the point I want to make is that the play illustrates Sartre's contention that freedom is difficult for humans to bear. It's not just, as Dostoevsky showed, that we value other things more than our freedom. The difficulty is that, because we are free, we have to accept responsibility for our actions. There is no one else to blame, only ourselves. Yet, even though human beings employ a variety of different strategies of Bad Faith, this uncomfortable truth cannot be avoided: it is we, and we alone, who bear responsibility for our actions.

But there is another, more contentious aspect to Sartre's account of why our freedom troubles us. To understand this line of thought, we need to recall Sartre's claim that both transcendence and facticity characterize human beings. His assertion that we are transcending beings is a way of registering our freedom to transform the circumstances of our existence – our facticity – and remake the world and ourselves in accordance with our own ideas. The problem is that, once we have done so, once we have acted in a transcending manner, we create a new facticity. But *this* facticity cannot be taken to be a necessary reflection of who we really are any more than our earlier one, for we still have the power to transcend it. On Sartre's view, our freedom – combined with our factical existence – condemns us to a restless existence in which we can never be satisfied with what we have accomplished.

At times, it seems that Sartre reaches this conclusion simply from an analysis of consciousness. In the last chapter, we saw that Sartre holds that every positional consciousness spawns a non-positional consciousness in which we are aware of the former. When I feel sad, say because Pierre never did meet me in the café, I am also conscious of feeling sad. But because I am conscious of feeling sad, I cannot 'inhabit' that feeling of sadness completely. As we might now put it, I distance myself from my own feeling. It's as if Sartre thought that becoming aware of what one was feeling entailed that one would feel alienated from that feeling, for one would see one's inhabiting of that feeling as a sort of act one was putting on. As Sartre puts it, 'The being-in-itself of sadness perpetually haunts my consciousness (of) being sad, but it is a value which I cannot realize' (*Being and Nothingness*, 104). Although we recognize and aspire to a state of being sad in-ourselves, we are 'haunted' by our inability to completely immerse ourselves in this – or any other – emotional state. Since it is in the nature of consciousness to be reflective, we can never fully inhabit any conscious state that we are in, so that our 'restlessness' lies in the very nature of our being.

It's not clear that Sartre is correct in his analysis of how reflection affects our emotional lives. While reflectively considering a state I am in may often cause me to be in a changed state of mind, it is not clear that this need always be the case. I was just feeling very happy when I was asked to do a radio interview. After a moment, I self-consciously observed that I was in that state. Is there anything that precludes me from simply accepting that that is the state I am in, rather than, as Sartre seems to suggest, retreating from a full embrace of it?

In any case, Sartre thinks that our self-consciousness contributes to the difficulty we have accepting our freedom, for it means that we always feel deficient, unable to fully inhabit any state that we are in. Although, as nihilating beings, we always have the opportunity to take actions by means of which we reinvent ourselves, we can never be satisfied with the results. Our awareness of our own freedom condemns us to live with the tension of having to make some-thing of ourselves and knowing that we can never fully be the being we make of ourselves – at least until our deaths.

Indeed, living as a free but factical being is so difficult that human beings have, during the course of history, developed a range of different ways to slough off responsibility for their actions. From Sartre's point of view, God is a prime example of such an evasion. Why? Because, although the idea of God fulfills other roles in religious belief that Sartre fails to give their due, the notion of God certainly provides human beings with a range of excuses for their actions. For example, in the Judeo–Christian tradition, God gives human beings a list of things they should not do: worship other gods, steal, commit adultery, and so on. Now in fact, there are many more commandments than just those ten. The Old Testament actually lists 613 commandments that determine virtually every aspect of a person's life. What can we say of a person who lives her life in accordance with them? Well, in one sense, she would be free when, for example, she refrains from shoplifting a dress because one of the Ten Commandments says that she should not steal. After all, she has made a choice about what to do. *But* there is another sense in which she is not fully realizing her freedom, because she does not have to decide which norms of conduct are the ones she will adhere to in living her life. Once she has chosen to live a life according to the Bible's commands, all moral rules are determined for her. She has no freedom to decide whether or not to obey them, for it is part and parcel of the religious life to follow *all* of those rules. So, even though the religious person remains conscious of being free to steal or not, she is not free to decide whether stealing itself is wrong, for that is determined by the eighth Commandment. For this reason, according to the Existentialists, she abdicates one aspect of her freedom as a human being.

The point is not just that the Existentialists – and here it is important to acknowledge once again that there are religious Existentialists as well – are hostile to traditional religion, but that they are interested in understanding how people benefit *existentially* from giving up control over their own lives. What the Existentialists conclude is that living a life in complete acknowledgment of our nature as humans is very difficult, if not impossible. As a result, we look for ways to avoid the burden of our own freedom and seek out structures that allow us to pretend to ourselves that we are free even as we use them to give up our freedom.

The Existentialists' account of the human ambivalence to our own freedom has an important corollary, for it provides an interesting perspective for assessing social practices and institutions. We can ask whether a given practice or institution that is part of our culture supports human freedom or whether it provides people with ways to escape from the difficulties involved in acknowledging their own freedom. In subsequent chapters, we shall explore this aspect of the Existentialists' theory of human freedom more specifically. But, before we get to that, metaphysics calls us once again ...

3
Others

So this is hell. I'd never have believed it. You remember all we were told about the torture-chambers, the fire and brimstone, the 'burning marl.' Old wives' tales! There's no need for red-hot pokers. Hell is – other people.

(*No Exit*, 46–7)

This dramatic statement, occurring near the end of Sartre's play *No Exit*, is spoken by Garcin, the journalist upset that others view him as a coward when he feels he has not yet had a chance to reveal his courageous nature. His words reflect his realization that being trapped for eternity with only Inez and Estelle for company is truly a terrible fate. But why is this? To most of us, having relationships with other people is one of the most important aspects of our lives, part of what gives our lives their meaning. And the thought of spending eternity with two women would bring a smile to the lips of many men. But Garcin is asserting that we are mistaken about our understanding of his situation, that our relationships with others are actually *hell*. Can this really be true? And, if so, how are we to assess his claim?

The goal of this chapter is to explain the philosophical basis for Garcin's claim, for it is, I believe, a pretty fair statement of Sartre's view of human relationships. But, in order to understand why Sartre thinks of our connections to other people in this way, we will have to take a long detour into the Existentialists' take on the existence of others. After doing so, we will return to Garcin with a great deal more understanding than we now possess.

Ever since Descartes (see text box opposite), Western philosophy has been bedeviled by two related philosophical problems that are both forms of skepticism. The first is labeled 'skepticism about the external world' and is based on the belief that we have immediate access only to the contents of our own minds or consciousnesses. The problem with this view is that we ordinarily believe in the existence of objects external to our minds, like the computer on which I am typing this sentence or the page on which you are reading it. However, if we have immediate access only to the contents of our own minds, as this view requires, how can we justify our belief in the existence of these 'external things'? Is there no real justification for thinking that there is a world of things 'out there,' that is, external to our own minds? According to this skeptical point of view, even our own bodies have a problematic status because they are not immediately recognizable as part of who or what we are. These views pose serious problems that philosophers working within the Cartesian tradition have to attempt to solve.

The second problem facing post-Cartesian philosophers concerns the existence of other people and, more specifically, their minds. Although we all believe that there are others besides ourselves in the world, it is not easy to say what justifies this belief. Even if we allow that we have knowledge of the existence of bodies in the world that resemble our own, the question remains as to our justification for believing that there are minds 'attached' to those bodies that are like our own minds in important ways. In the case of our own minds, we know that they exist precisely because of the 'privileged access' we have to them. The claim is that we generally know directly what the contents of our own mind are. But this direct knowledge is precisely what we lack in the case of other people's minds, to which we cannot have such direct and immediate access. Thus, the skeptical problem of other minds is how to justify our ordinary belief in the reality of them.

René Descartes (1596–1650) is generally regarded as the father of modern Western philosophy. This is because he considered issues of knowledge (epistemology) to precede questions about the nature of reality (metaphysics). This was quite a change, since metaphysics had, since Aristotle, been seen as 'first philosophy,' or the most basic aspect of philosophical investigation.

Descartes employed the technique of methodological skepticism in order to call into question the validity of all the accepted sources of human knowledge, from sense perception to mathematics. Rather than attempting to prove that these sources were incapable of providing certain knowledge, Descartes rejected them whenever he could find a reason to doubt their accuracy.

Instead of sense perception and common sense, Descartes considered *reason* to be the sole, accurate guide to reality. This was because he believed God placed reason and its 'natural light' within each of us in order for us to have access to the truth about the world.

Descartes' philosophy is characterized by a number of dualisms, the most important of which is that between mind and body. According to Descartes, the truth of the famous *Cogito* argument – 'I think, therefore I am' – is that I am identical with my mind. Although I have an incredibly close relationship to my body – so close that I form a 'unit' with it, according to Descartes – it is not an essential part of my being, but only something in which I find myself temporarily housed.

One of the legacies that Descartes bequeathed to the Western philosophical tradition, then, was this set of two skeptical problems. Virtually every succeeding major philosopher after him had to find a way to resolve each of them, and they sought to do so in various different ways. For example, Bishop Berkeley (1685–1753), the Irish idealist philosopher, hewed an unlikely path. Berkeley accepted the skeptical claim that we only have knowledge of our immediate perceptions, yet denied that this meant we did not have knowledge of the existence of other minds. Additionally, he argued that physical objects do not exist if we mean by that term ongoing objects that exist independently of our perception of them. Paradoxical as this view sounds on first hearing it, Berkeley argued that it was really the commonsensical thing to think.

Berkeley was an Empiricist, because he thought that our sense perceptions are a more accurate guide to the nature of reality than our reason. (The Rationalists took the other option, seeing our reason as more suitable to truth than our senses are.) Like all the Empiricists, he had a hard time *justifying* our belief in the existence of other minds. A Rationalist, such as Baruch Spinoza (1632–1677), had an easier time providing a solution to this skeptical dilemma. Spinoza thought that we can have knowledge that there are other minds in the world, but only because these minds are part of a single overarching substance. Spinoza called this substance *Deus sive Natura*, God or Nature, thereby indicating two of the infinite ways in which this substance can be understood: either as mind or as matter. On this monistic account of reality (a monist believes in the existence of only one type of substance in the world), we humans are part of a greater whole, so that once we attain the correct philosophical outlook, one that relies on reason rather than sense perception, we attain knowledge of the existence of both the human mind and the human body, as 'modes' of the existence of this one, overarching substance, *Deus sive Natura*.

Even though philosophical positions such as those of Berkeley and Spinoza seem extremely odd and counter-intuitive to most people, it is hard to refute them philosophically. Furthermore, it just is not clear whether their anti-Cartesian positions had more to recommend them than Descartes' skeptically infused position. After all, if the price of denying skepticism was to dismiss the existence of physical objects or admit besides mind and matter, infinitely many additional ways of conceiving reality, it became unclear which was worse: the disease of Cartesianism or its Berkeleyan or Spinozan cures!

In this light, we can understand why Heidegger's *Being and Time* had such a huge impact on the philosophical community at the time of its publication. For in it, Heidegger undertook a fundamental reassessment of the plausibility of skepticism as a philosophical problem. In doing so, he attempted to show that both forms of skepticism that the Western tradition had inherited from Descartes were based upon a mistaken understanding of the nature of humans' experience of the world. As a result, Heidegger thought these skeptical positions needed to be avoided rather than solved.

Heidegger's strategy in regard to each of the forms of skepticism was the same: to show that the model of our epistemic situation that Descartes employed was fundamentally misguided. To accomplish this, he presented an alternative and, he believed, more adequate account of what it is to be a human creature living in a world inhabited by others. On Heidegger's picture of what our experience is like, the two forms of skepticism cannot even be coherently formulated. So, instead of trying to *solve* these twin problems, Heidegger aimed to *dis-solve* them, to make it impossible to frame them coherently and thus to eliminate their allure.

Dis-solving skepticism

So let's look more carefully at Heidegger's 'dis-solution' of the problem of skepticism with regard to other minds in order to better understand his alternative understanding of our experience. In arguing for his position, the skeptic asserts that we have direct access to the contents of our own minds and thus know that our minds exist. This is the point of Descartes' 'I think, therefore I am.' But this is just what we lack in the case of others, for we are ontologically barred from having direct access to their minds. The skeptic asserts, then, that our claim to know that others have minds relies on a problematic inference from our own case to that of others. He points out that we cannot really ever know that there are minds 'attached' to the bodies that we see 'out there' that look similar to our own. As a result, we cannot have knowledge of the existence of minds other than our own (and, possibly, God's).

The traditional route to solving this problem involves an argument from analogy. The skeptic concedes three things: first, that we have knowledge of the contents of our own minds; second, that our minds are so intimately related to 'our' bodies that we can, for most purposes, treat the two as one composite entity; and, third, that we have knowledge of the existence of bodies that resemble our own. What the skeptic denies, however, is that we have knowledge of the existence of minds that are as intimately linked to their corresponding bodies as our minds are linked to our own bodies.

In contrast, the traditional anti-skeptical response claims that our knowledge of the existence of other minds is based on an analogy. Because we each see that other bodies behave much like our own body does and because in our own case we know that our body behaves as it does because it is controlled by a mind – indeed, our own – we can infer the existence of other minds attached to other bodies in the same way as our mind is attached to our own body.

Of course, the skeptic is not satisfied by this. He responds that, while we may make such an inference, it does not provide us with certain *knowledge*. For example, I have no grounds for ruling out the possibility that I am the only human with a mind. Every human body that I see, including my own, could be nothing but a computer projection. (Think, here, of the original *Matrix* film!) Since this is possible – although, of course, highly unlikely and itself plagued with many problems – I am not justified, according to the skeptic, in believing in the existence of other minds who control the behavior of the human bodies I perceive any more than I have justification for thinking of them as controlled by a super-computer.

Heidegger's response to the dialectic of this debate between the skeptic and the anti-skeptic in regard to other minds was to argue that we should not be looking for a better way to support an inference to the existence of other minds, as many philosophers had previously attempted. Instead, he proposed that we should contest the very basis of skepticism: the claim that our knowledge of the existence of others is fundamentally different from our knowledge of ourselves. As part of this effort, Heidegger rejected the dualistic framework of bodies and minds that he believed inevitably resulted in skeptical doubts and proposed that we would do better to think of ourselves as *embodied experiencers of a world that we share with others like ourselves.* Once we do so, the primary philosophical question becomes one of discerning the necessary features our experience has, a philosophical task that Heidegger thought the great German philosopher Immanuel Kant had correctly formulated but failed to answer adequately.

Recall that Heidegger used the word *Dasein* (German for 'being there') to refer to humans. Now, in the present context, we can appreciate an additional rationale for what might have previously seemed an odd philosophical term. By calling us *Dasein*, Heidegger replaces the dualistic scheme of humans as minds conjoined to bodies with a monistic conception in which humans are necessarily embodied creatures existing in the midst of a world. Heidegger's use of the term *Dasein* attempts to make it impossible for us to think of ourselves as 'consciousnesses' who are problematically 'attached' to the real world of physical things and other people. Heidegger's claim in regard to skepticism about the existence of other minds – and note how the very language with which the problem is formulated gets undercut by

Heidegger's terminology – is that part of what it is to be a *Dasein* is to exist in a world *with* other *Dasein*s existing alongside oneself. In other words, *Dasein*'s way of *being-in-the-world* is always *being-with* (*Mitsein*).

Yet, how does Heidegger justify his claim that *Dasein* exists in a world populated by other *Dasein*s? Remember, the phenomenological method that the Existentialists employ demands that the philosopher supplement her abstract claim with the description of an experience that allows the truth of the claim to emerge clearly. To provide this, Heidegger asks us to consider how we encounter things in the course of our everyday experience. When we pose the question in this way, the answer seems obvious: the things we encounter in our ordinary dealings are *useful items*, rather than the abstract structures that Descartes and others took them to be. When I encounter a chair, for example, I take it to be a thing for sitting, not a four-legged object with a horizontal slab attached to a vertical piece. The chair's physical structure is less important to its being a chair than the fact that it plays the role of something upon which one can sit. We encounter the chair as a thing that fulfills a function rather than as a three-dimensional object with a certain geometric structure.

But a chair's being a 'useful-for-sitting-thing' rather than a 'four-legged-entity-with-a-certain-structure' is only one aspect of the being that a chair has for me in my daily life. When I encounter a chair, I don't think of it as existing *for me*, even though I think of it as having a function that is useful to me. Instead, I take it to be something on which *one* sits, that is, a for-sitting-thing that *anyone* could avail themselves of when in its vicinity. This seemingly trivial claim has, according to Heidegger, important philosophical consequences. He claims that it is through our interactions with everyday things such as tables and chairs that we first encounter other humans, for we realize that it is part of our experience of the world that it be populated by other humans, other *Dasein*s. Why? Because there are things that I encounter in my world – implements (*Zeug*) – that bear the traces of those others who made them in such a way that they can fulfill a need of those who come across them. But then other humans are simply part of the world we inhabit, so that it does not make sense to put our knowledge of their existence on a different and more problematic basis than our knowledge of our own existence. *Dasein*'s world is, simply put, a world populated with other *Dasein*s. For this reason, Heidegger conceptualizes it as a *with-world*.

Like all the Existentialists, Heidegger defended his philosophical claims in ways that were unusual for a philosopher. So, as part of his case for the validity of the notion of a 'with-world,' he gave a rather surprising interpretation of Vincent Van Gogh's well-known painting *Shoes*. The painting consists of a pair of worn work shoes, such as a peasant might wear, sitting on the ground with untied laces, as if discarded after a day's work. In a striking analysis of the painting, Heidegger claims that these shoes reveal the *world* of the peasant woman to whom he says the shoes belong:

> From the dark opening of the worn insides of the shoes the toilsome tread of the worker stares forth … In the shoes vibrates the silent call of the earth, its quiet gift of ripening grain and its unexpected self-refusal in the fallow desolation of the wintry field … This equipment belongs to the *earth*, and it is protected in the *world* of the peasant woman … By virtue of this reliability the peasant woman is made privy to the silent call of the earth; by virtue of the reliability of the equipment she is sure of her world. ('The Origin of the Work of Art,' 158–9)

On Heidegger's interpretation, Van Gogh's painting reveals a great deal more than the mere existence of the peasant woman to whom these shoes belong. Though the painting does do that, thereby undermining skepticism about the existence of other minds, it also gives us access to her *world*, with its cares and concerns, as well as to the role of the shoes in allowing her to create a space for herself within that world. For that reason, according to Heidegger, Van Gogh's masterpiece illustrates how our experience is one of a world populated by other people. We no longer have reason to think that we must infer their existence from the movements of their bodies or from analogies to ourselves, as the Cartesian asserts.

In his discussion of *Shoes*, Heidegger uses the concept of *world* in a way that is characteristic of the Existentialist tradition and that will be important for what follows. Rather than treating 'world' as referring to a material structure such as that a physicist might contemplate, Heidegger uses it to refer to the entire complex of relationships to other entities, human and not, that a *Dasein* has. Heidegger thus speaks of 'the world of the peasant woman,' referring to her cares, her tool, the gift of grain, and so on. All of these make up her world. Thus, this new sense of *world* relativizes the concept to the human whose world it is and who stands at its origin.

If Heidegger is correct in his contentions about how we experience the existence of others, then the entire framework of Cartesianism is overturned. What is often called Cartesianism's 'Robinson Crusoe' epistemological position is fundamentally misguided, for we are not alone. The world in which we live is a world that we share with others who are like us and of whose existence we can be sure.

Let me interject a note here. One of the remarkable things about the history of Western philosophy is the split, occurring during the twentieth century, in the manner in which philosophy was generally practiced in Continental Europe and in English speaking countries as well as Austria. In the twentieth century, Continental philosophy and Analytic philosophy, as these two modes are known, developed in relative isolation from each other. Yet, despite their lack of interaction, there is an important similarity between the fundamental critique that

Heidegger made of the Cartesian tradition from within the Continental tradition and that made by Ludwig Wittgenstein (1889–1951) from within the Analytic tradition. Both Heidegger and Wittgenstein thought that the dualisms ruling Western philosophy had to be undone and, in rather different ways, they both set out to do so. We have already seen how Heidegger attempted to introduce a new set of philosophical terms, such as *Dasein*, that would undermine the temptation to view the world dualistically. In his *Philosophical Investigations* (1953), Wittgenstein focused on social practices, most centrally that of learning and using a language, with a similar intent: to replace the traditional assumptions of Western philosophy with a view of human beings as shaped in the most basic ways by their engagement in social interactions.

The *They*

In any event, Heidegger does not end his analysis of the role of others in *Dasein's* world with the contention that we experience others as part of our world. He continues by posing a question that at first seems nonsensical. *Who* are these *Dasein*s that we both are and encounter in our world? His surprising answer is: these *Dasein*s are a *They*.

Before you throw down this book in exasperation, let me try to explain in simple terms what Heidegger is contending. First, a linguistic note: the German term that is translated as 'the They' is *das Man*. This is a nominalization (i.e., another part of speech, in this case a pronoun, that is turned into a noun) of a normal German expression, *man* (with a small 'm'). Usually, *man* would be translated as 'one.' When children are taught how to behave, we often tell them how *one* is to behave, as when, for example, I tell my son, 'That's not how *one* holds a fork.' The German translation of this sentence is, 'So hält *man* die Gabel nicht.'

When we use this locution, the word 'one' refers to how people are generally expected to do something. It invokes a norm or standard of behavior that holds within a community and asserts that members of the community are simply to conform to that norm or standard. If you look at the first sketch of a fork in a person's hand below, you see an example of how *one* does *not* hold a fork. Of course, this does not mean that one could not hold a fork in this way, only that this is not the way that *we* do it.

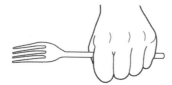

Figure 1 How one does not hold a fork

On the other hand, the second drawing shows the proper way for one to hold a fork (or one of them, at least), a way that conforms to the norms that *we* have set for proper fork-holding behavior.

Figure 2 How one holds a fork

On Heidegger's view, saying that the others we encounter exist in the mode of a They or a One is to say that they are part of a community that imposes standards on individual *Dasein*s that specify how a *Dasein* is to behave. In other words, to be a *Dasein* is to find oneself a member of a community of *Dasein*s that promulgates standards for behavior.

Since I mentioned Wittgenstein earlier, it's worth noting that, from his point of view, this is a very significant claim that is best illustrated by language acquisition. We do not come into the world able to speak a language, even if we do have innate capacities that make our doing so possible. In order for us to become competent users of a language, there must be language-users who can illustrate the proper uses of the language. We become proficient at speaking a language because of a community of language-users who introduce us to the norms of how *one* speaks.

All this seems pretty unremarkable until we combine it with an Existentialist theme we previously encountered. Recall the view of human beings discussed in the first chapter as characteristic of Existentialism. There, I emphasized the importance that the Existentialists gave to freedom: it was the primary value in human life for the Existentialists. So, for example, Sartre claimed that humans were essentially *nihilating* beings, creatures who were able to structure their own behavior instead of being determined by nature to behave in pre-established ways.

What happens when a nihilating being encounters others in the form of a They? The They expects that the encountering person will conform to Their standards of behavior. Although I first illustrated the notion of a They with the relatively trivial example of table manners, the *They* extends its presence into virtually all aspects of a person's life. Just think of all the different ways in which you have felt the pressure to conform to standards that others have set, but that you did not feel comfortable with. Take how we dress. I am someone who hates wearing ties, for I don't like the feel of them wrapped tightly around my neck. Nonetheless, when I began to teach virtually all of my colleagues wore ties and sport coats. I did not want to do the same, and for more reasons than just my physical comfort. I also thought of ties as conveying a false sense of who I wanted to be as a teacher. Yet there was a lot of pressure on me to conform to how the other members of the philosophy department dressed. Wearing ties was simply what *one* did as a faculty member at a premier university, as one of my smaller-minded colleagues repeatedly reminded me. If I was to be one of Them, I was expected to conform. This was the message that I frequently received, although not always in such an explicit manner. Many other, subtler suggestions conveyed to me the message that there was a standard for dress that would be enforced and to which I was expected to adhere. The philosophical moral here is that the 'dominance of the They,' as Heidegger terms it, forces us to give up our freedom to live as we choose in favor of accepting those modes of being that accord with the standards set by a specific community of others. In place of our capacity to be free initiators of actions, our initial encounters with others influence us to become conformists, and, consequently, we are pushed to behave in ways that are socially acceptable. As Heidegger says, under the dominance of the They, 'Everyone is the other, and no one is himself' (*Being and Time*, 165).

'The look'

Thus far, our examination into our relationship with others has turned out to be quite different than we first expected. Initially, granting that our world was a 'with-world' promised liberation from the problems of Cartesian skepticism. That is, the phenomenological account of how we come into contact with others undercut the Cartesian privileging of our own selves that had resulted in skepticism. But now, in place of the liberating feeling that resulted from jettisoning the problematic metaphysics and epistemology of Cartesianism, we find ourselves with the depressing sense that others enforce social conformity by getting us to behave as they want us to rather than as we would like. Although we will move beyond this point of view in a moment, for now we must plunge into it more deeply.

Heidegger's analysis of being-with and the They influenced Sartre's account of others and their effect on our existence. But Sartre rejects Heidegger's account of an initial, positive understanding that we have of others sharing our world with us and offers an unremittingly bleak and negative view of the role that others play in our lives. From Sartre's point of view, others take our freedom from us, just as we take it from them. This account of our relationships with others as inherently competitive and destructive challenges Heidegger's account by denying that our relationships with others are initially free of conflict. Still, Sartre does admit that, from a formal point of view, there is a third aspect to existence that his account of the *in-itself* and the *for-itself* neglected: the *for-another*. By acknowledging that existence (or being) includes a third ontological dimension, Sartre's account of others functions to further enhance the metaphysical structure of existence itself by acknowledging that it includes a new ontological category: the 'for-another.'

In order to show that this way of being is part of the structure of our human world, Sartre proceeds in an almost novelistic manner, launching into a phenomenological description of jealousy. What happens when we are jealous? Many accounts of the emotions treat them as feeling states, usually ones that are 'directed towards' a specific object. So, if I am jealous of my lover, I have a specific feeling toward her, one that pains me because I think that she is unfaithful. But Sartre thinks that such an account of jealousy is inadequate. Jealousy – and all other emotions – structure our lives in a more fundamental way. Sartre proposes that an emotion such as jealousy *colors* our entire world.

In literature, the classic portrayal of jealousy is Shakespeare's *Othello*. Iago suggests to Othello, a much acclaimed general and warrior, that his wife, Desdemona, is having an affair with Cassio, one of his lieutenants. Once Othello hears Iago's suggestion, he is completely possessed by the jealousy it arouses, and his entire world becomes oriented around that emotion. Every object becomes a sign he tries to interpret in order to confirm his suspicions. So a misplaced handkerchief tragically becomes a sign of betrayal. Othello is so dominated by his jealousy that it permeates everything he sees. His world becomes a projection of his jealousy, with, of course, devastating results.

How does this bear on the question of the existence of others? Sartre asks us to imagine a person who, like Othello, is completely overcome with jealousy. Because he is worried that his lover is betraying him, he behaves in ways that we recognize as symptoms of jealousy. He paces the floor nervously, wondering where his lover is. He then decides that he needs to know what is happening, so he peeks through the keyhole of the door to his lover's room in an attempt to see if she is being unfaithful. Like Othello, while the lover is possessed by jealousy, his entire world is oriented around that emotion. Various things that he sees, like, say, a discarded blouse, become indications of unfaithfulness. His emotion colors his whole world by providing the interpretive framework within which everything he sees is placed.

Suddenly, the lover peeking through the keyhole hears a footstep: 'There must be someone coming down the hall. They'll see me. Oh no! What will they think of me? They won't understand why I'm here. I look so foolish, face pressed to the door. What can I do?' These are the sorts of thoughts we can imagine the jealous lover having. Sartre's startling claim is that we have just witnessed a radical transformation in the lover's existence as a result of his presumption that the footsteps he hears indicate he has been seen. Instead of inhabiting a world of which he is the origin – as he did when he was consumed by jealousy, for he took everything as signs to confirm his own emotion – he now exists within a world whose origin is that *other* who is looking at him. That is, at least in his imagination, the man now sees himself as the other would see him, as just one of an entire ensemble of beings in that other's world. The other is, as an independent being, the source of his own world and so the lover is consigned to a position within that world. He becomes just another *thing* in the other's world. Not only has his existence been *stolen* by the other, but he himself has been reduced to the status of a mere object in that other's world. Thus, in this way, he is subject to a double objectification or reification.

The precise way in which the lover responds to the presence of the other is not important. He might experience very different emotions, such as embarrassment or anger, depending on his situation. What is significant, however, is that he no longer exists as he did previously, for his awareness of being seen changes the nature of his existence. He becomes aware of the existence of the other as the bearer of what Sartre calls 'the look.' Although we first encounter other people as elements of our world, this experience of assuming that we are being observed by another brings forth another dimension: I lose both my world and also my self when I encounter the other. It does not matter if the lover is mistaken about the presence of another consciousness perceiving him. Sartre's point is that part of the structure of consciousness is that it can conceptualize itself as an object of another's perception. In other words, *objectification* is part of the being of consciousness.

This theme of the other as a threat to our existence can be traced back to G.W.F. Hegel's discussion of 'Self-Consciousness' in his *Phenomenology of Spirit* (see text box, p. 65.)

Although Hegel was one of the philosophers whom the Existentialists criticized for attempting to build a rational picture of the world, he also deeply influenced them. Sartre's account of the impact that others have on our world is a direct descendent of Hegel's life-and-death struggle, in which a consciousness experiences the brute existence of another consciousness as a threat to its existence and thus seeks to annihilate it. But, unlike Sartre, Hegel thought that such conflictual relationships with others could be resolved in a 'higher synthesis' that fostered cooperation. So although Hegel's claim that human beings are constituted through their encounter with others remains a basic presumption of Existentialist thinking, the Existentialists denied that social cooperation was necessarily the solution to the dilemmas posed by the existence of others.

Sartre drew another important consequence from our experience of being the object of the 'look' of an other: it is this experience that constitutes me as an *ego*, that is, a being with a fixed nature. When I am being looked at by another, the other sees me as an object, a being in-itself with a definite essence, a certain type of person, perhaps, as in the case we have been considering of the jealous lover. But when I am seen in this way, my being is fixed and determined. It is as if I lose the ability to control my own fate, one of the central characteristics that the Existentialists posit as at the heart of our being. For this reason, Sartre characterizes this experience as one in which 'my transcendence [is] transcended' (*Being and Nothingness*, 352). In other words, we are no longer beings of mere possibilities. We have acquired a determinate nature. Heidegger terms the self that has emerged from our encounter with others a 'They-self,' in order to indicate how deeply the presence of others injects itself into the core of our being.

Sartre's account of others thus results in a very different view of the role that others play in our lives than that we found developed by Heidegger. Sartre rejects any positive dimension to

Georg Wilhelm Friedrich Hegel (1770–1831) advocated a philosophical position he characterized as absolute idealism. This metaphysical view was intended to be a synthesis of rationalism and empiricism. It was rationalist because it took all of reality to be an expression of the rationality of what Hegel termed the Idea. It was empiricist because it attempted to provide an encyclopedic grasp of empirical reality, incorporating the results of contemporary scientific theorizing as well as actual historical developments.

Most influential on the Existentialists was Hegel's early book, *The Phenomenology of Spirit* (1807). Written from the point of view of 'consciousness,' this work attempts to show that there is an inevitable course that consciousness takes from its beginnings in 'Sense Certainty' until it reaches the stage of 'Absolute Knowledge.' Although the Existentialists rejected Hegel's attempt to present a single, comprehensive perspective from which to view all of human history, they were deeply affected by his *dialectical* conception of history. On Hegel's view, every specific way of approaching the world and each stage in world history gets transcended because it has within itself the seeds of its own destruction. But this is not a purely negative process, according to Hegel, for a new synthesis always emerges, and the process continues until it reaches the final stage of Absolute Knowledge, when no further development is necessary.

Hegel's 'mature' work, an attempt to spell out his conception of the basic structure of reality, was presented in his *Encyclopedia of the Philosophical Sciences* (1816). This work is more abstract and less tied to human experience than the *Phenomenology*. Thus, the *Encyclopedia* exerted less influence on the Existentialists' thinking. For them, Hegel's immersion in the flux of experience in the *Phenomenology* was more significant than his abstract articulation of the categories of being in the *Encyclopedia* and other works written from the standpoint of Absolute Knowledge, the final, settled worldview Hegel believed himself to have attained.

human sociality and dismisses the notion that we are able to comprehend the other as another self. For Sartre, my primary experience of the other is as the cause of my objectification, the loss of my being, as I am placed into the *other's* world. When I attempt to regain my self, I do so by objectifying the other, for only in so far as I succeed in doing so, will I succeed in regaining *my* world. We are thus condemned to a metaphysical struggle with the other, in which any victory remains temporary, for the other is simultaneously engaged in an attempt to regain *his* own being, which he has lost through his interaction with me.

One of the most important and insightful features of Sartre's philosophy arises as an extension of the analysis of the impact that others have on the human being. Because we initially experience the other as a threat to ourselves in so far as the other 'steals' our world, we enter into what Sartre called *concrete* relations with others in which we attempt to recapture both ourselves and our worlds from the other's intervention. Although Sartre thinks that these attempts are doomed to failure, his registering actual forms of human relationship within an ontological account of our nature brought philosophy into a more intimate relationship with real lived lives than previous – and many subsequent – philosophers had managed to achieve.

The concrete relationships that Sartre considers in *Being and Nothingness* include love, desire, masochism, and sadism. In each case, he shows that the attempt to use this specific manner of interacting with another human being fails to realize a person's aim of restoring their sense of selfhood. For example, Sartre discusses sex under the rubric of *desire* (the French word, *désir*, has a sexual connotation). Sartre tells us that desire takes as its object the body of the other and that one must make oneself *flesh* in order to appropriate the other's flesh. The basic vehicle for the expression of desire, he claims, is the *caress*, in which the other is made incarnate through a manner of touching that registers in their body and brings about a sexual response. But, Sartre tells us, desire is itself doomed to failure. The problem is that the caress brings about pleasure, so that the other disappears as one enjoys oneself and focuses on one's own incarnation, one's own embodiment.

Sartre's actual discussion of sex/desire is a lot more explicit than this and involves a discussion of, among other things, sexual intercourse. Sartre's emphasis on intercourse reveals a heterosexist bias in his thought as well as a masculinist one. Nonetheless, his attempt to show that a variety of forms of human experience need to be placed within the ontological framework of the human being's quest for selfhood opened up a new way of thinking about the philosophical implications of human experience.

Sartre's view of desire and other concrete human relationships was also heavily dependent upon Hegel's philosophical framework. Hegel posited a drive toward mutual recognition as essential to consciousness' drive to attain certainty of itself. Thus, he was the first philosopher to provide a means for integrating actual modes of human relationships into an ontological account of the human being. In the *Phenomenology*, Hegel placed a range of human experiences – including slavery, war, and religious faith – into his progressive account of spirit's attempt to know itself. He argued that each attempt that consciousness made to achieve autonomy was doomed, but that it led inevitably to another such attempt until, in the end, a satisfactory mode of experience was achieved, namely Absolute (or philosophical) Knowledge.

Sartre and the Existentialists thus took from Hegel this commitment to integrate into philosophy our human experience of trying to make sense of a world into which we are thrust. Their distinctive contribution, however, was to reject Hegel's view that there was only one correct way of coping with the problems posed by our existence. By stressing the *individuality* of human beings, the Existentialists sought to make philosophy responsive to each person's freedom to choose how he or she would solve the issues with which all are confronted.

Is hell other people?

We are now prepared to return to the question with which I began this chapter: why does Garcin claim in *No Exit* that hell is other people? You will recall that the play concerns three people who are placed into a room with only each other for all eternity. This setting allows Sartre a graphic realization of his contention about human relationships: that purely dyadic (two-termed) relationships are impossible, for we are always aware of the possibility of being observed by a third person, the 'other' who takes us out of our primary ways of being. As a result, it is impossible for anyone to fully inhabit any emotion or role, something we earlier saw Sartre derive from the nature of consciousness itself, for once one becomes aware that one is in a certain state, one no longer fully inhabits that state. So consider Garcin's attempt to make love to Estelle, a young and attractive woman – and thus achieve a state of complete 'being.' The lesbian Inez intervenes:

> Very well, have it your own way. I'm the weaker party, one against two. But don't forget I'm here, and watching. I shan't take my eyes off you, Garcin; when you're kissing her, you'll feel them boring into you. Yes, have it your own way, make love and get it over. We're in hell; my turn will come. (*No Exit*, 35–6)

Of course, with Inez watching, Garcin is unable to make love to Estelle, for Inez's look makes him conscious that he appears to her as the absurd lover of the superficial Estelle. Instead of being absorbed in the passion of the moment, he is quite literally *self*-conscious, that is, aware of what he is doing. Thus unable to remain absorbed in his own world, Garcin is swept into *Inez's world* in which he appears in a shameful position similar to that of Sartre's jealous lover. Put another way, the presence of Inez results in Garcin's nihilating his relationship with Estelle.

This explains why Sartre thinks that 'hell is other people': Their look pulls us out of our own world and turns us into an object in theirs. As a result, our projects take on a different feel for us. We can no longer be content with them as they are, having become incapable of embracing them as meaningful. Instead, we not only acquire a self-consciousness that makes us doubt their validity, but are also unable to be fully present within them. We are condemned to vacillate between engagement in our world and a self-conscious withdrawal from it. Others thus bring consciousness' own fragility to a new level of instability.

But this is not Sartre's or the Existentialists' final word on our relationships with others or on the options for us as humans, although it does represent a crucial aspect of their thought. A first question we might be prompted to ask is why we allow others to absorb us into the They. We'll seek to answer this question in the next chapter.

4
Anxiety

Over the course of the last three chapters, a complex picture has emerged of what the world of humans is like according to the Existentialists. They claim that the most important fact about us humans is that we are free, that nothing determines who we are or what we do. Yet, in presenting their account of the role of others in human life, the Existentialists claimed that we acquire a determinate sense of ourselves in a debased form, one in which we are less free spirits than conformists whose behavior fits into stereotyped patterns.

The puzzle that these twin theses raise is how human beings can exist-in-the-world in a manner that is in touch with their deepest potentials as individuals. Because the first experiences in which humans come to have any sense of who they are involve others through whose eyes they see themselves and whose standards determine how they shall act, it seems as if humans are precluded from living lives that are constructed on the basis of what might truly fulfill them. So our lives would seem to be inherently *inauthentic*.

An additional puzzle arises because our account has not made it clear how, in the view of the Existentialists, human beings can have an adequate conception of themselves, for, on the account presented so far, we experience ourselves initially only through the alienating eyes of others. But if this were our only means of access to ourselves, the sorts of philosophical works that characterize Existentialism – works that attempt to spell out the nature of being human – could not be written. Clearly, this can't be right. There must be some way for humans to acquire an adequate conception of the type of creature that they are.

The key to humans discovering their own nature, according to the Existentialists, is *anxiety*. In 1947, W.H. Auden published a poem called *The Age of Anxiety*, which won the Pulitzer Prize for Poetry the following year. In many ways, it seemed to capture the spirit of that time, in particular by characterizing the period as one in which the predominant emotion was that of anxiety. There are many reasons why people living in the wake of World War II might have responded to the notion that anxiety was the emotion of their 'age,' not the least of which were the existence of the atomic bomb and the threat of nuclear annihilation that it brought in its wake.

For the Existentialists, however, the pervasiveness of anxiety is less a reflection of the times and its specific occurrences than a feature of human existence itself. For them, anxiety is not just one emotion among others: it is the one that best reveals to us our nature as human beings. This means that anxiety has metaphysical significance: it allows humans to correctly under-stand the nature of the being that they are, but only if they have a full and complete experience of this emotion. For many people, anxiety is an emotion from which they flee, seeking in various ways to anesthetize themselves to its unpleasantness. But the Existentialists believe that paying attention to one's anxiety is crucial because of the significance of what it signals.

In order to understand what the Existentialists think the role anxiety plays is, it will be useful to begin by thinking about what characterizes anxiety as a specific emotion. To do so, it will be useful to compare anxiety to another emotion with which it shares many traits: worry. Consider how you might respond to a friend who says that she is anxious. One response might be to say, 'What are you worried about? You have nothing to be concerned about,' thereby treating her anxiety as if it were just a case of worry. A familiar dictionary definition of anxiety also assimilates it to worry: 'a subject or concern that causes worry.'

One reason why it is tempting to assimilate anxiety to worry is that both these emotions involve the presence of similar physiological characteristics. These include increased heart rate, speedier breathing, and flushing of the face. In addition, both are unpleasant emotions, emotions that we generally avoid if we can. So what distinguishes them from one other?

Worry is the more ordinary or, as contemporary philosophers say, 'garden-variety' emotion. Worry is characterized by its *intentionality*, that is, when I am worried, there is always something about which I am worried, some 'object' which is the focus of my concern. In some cases, it is a physical object, as when I'm worried that a bear might stumble into my campsite; but it can also be a psychic one, as my worry that the pain in my side will return. In the latter case, the object of the worry – the pain or its return – is not a physical but a psychological reality, though this does not make the pain or my worry about it any less real. And in both cases, the target of my worry is not merely the thing – be it the bear or the pain – but some future event: the bear's entry into my campsite or the pain returning.

Anxiety, on the other hand, is an emotion that psychologists generally characterize as 'free-floating.' What they mean by this is that there is no obvious object toward which anxiety is directed. To see the significance of this fact, consider the difference between a student's saying she is worried about a test she has to take and saying that she is anxious about it. If she is worried about the test, it might be because she is scared that she will fail it or get a grade lower than she wants or needs. In this case, there is a specific outcome of which she is afraid that forms the object of her worry. (Of course, there might be more than one, but this does not affect the point. We can just treat the conjunction of all those outcomes as the 'object' of the worry.) But when the test makes her anxious, she generally would be hard pressed to explain what about the test is making her feel that way. There is nothing specific that worries her – or else she would be feeling worried and not anxious. Anxiety has the peculiarity that it doesn't seem to be about anything! And yet it is at least as upsetting an emotion as worry and maybe even more so, particularly since it's so hard to figure out what is making one anxious.

Sartre's philosophical novel *Nausea*, is all about this emotion, although he calls it 'nausea' rather than anxiety. The hero of the novel, Antoine Roquentin, whom we already met earlier next to a tree in the park, is pervaded by this unsettling emotion, making it hard for him to pursue his chosen task, writing a biography of a minor figure in the French Revolution. Because of the peculiar nature of anxiety, the cause of his emotional state is not apparent to him, so he begins to keep a journal in which he records his experiences.

Many philosophers accept an intentional account of psychological states, according to which these states need to have an object, something they are 'about.' If this view is correct, then anxiety, as an emotion, must also be about something. But we have just seen that it does not appear to have an object, or else it would just resolve itself into ordinary, garden-variety worry. How can this puzzle about the nature of anxiety be resolved?

The tension between our analysis of anxiety as objectless and the thesis of intentionality is an example of an apparent contradiction. What this means is that it *appears* at first glance that both of these contentions cannot be true. Part of the philosophers' job is to provide some way of resolving such problematic situations. The strategy that is adopted by philosophers most of the time is to propose a theory that resolves the contradiction. They do this, for example, by showing that the two views that seem to contradict each other do not really do so, so there is no real contradiction at all. One of the unique features of Existentialism is that it often embraces paradox. But in regard to the issue confronting us now concerning anxiety, most Existentialists adopt the more usual strategy of trying to find a way out that makes sense to us.

They put forward a view of anxiety that makes sense of its unusual characteristics and that shows that its apparent object-lessness does not contradict the thesis of the intentionality of the mental states.

Anxiety's object

So let's think some more about what is going on in the example of the student feeling anxious about taking a test. What could such anxiety be *about*? As we have seen, if we want to maintain the distinction between worry and anxiety – and there does seem to be something unique about anxiety as an emotion that justifies not assimilating it to worry – then the anxiety she feels in regard to the test cannot be about any specific outcome, such as the possibility that she could fail it. Whatever this anxiety is about, it must be something much more general than failing the test or revealing how little she knows about the subject, for those outcomes are occasions for worry rather than anxiety.

Freudian psychology provides one way of understanding anxiety that presents a resolution of the apparent contradiction. From a psychoanalytic perspective, anxiety is really a form of worry, only the object of one's worry is unconscious, something of which one is not aware. This explains why anxiety appears to be objectless. Of course, the goal of psychoanalysis is, among other things, to make conscious those things in one's unconscious that are causing one anxiety or distress. The outcome of the process of analysis is to disarm one's anxieties by showing one their real objects.

So in the case of the student's anxiety about the test, a possible Freudian explanation is that she is worried that she will fail the test and she has an unconscious belief that her parents will reject her, withhold their love, if she does. Because of this unconscious belief, her (we shall assume) very reasonable worry about the outcome of the test gets overlaid with a quite unrealistic anxiety that is actually an unconscious fear. (Such unconscious beliefs, because they are unrealistic, can occur at any age. Indeed, their occurrence in unrealistic contexts is what makes neurotic behavior so aberrant.) Anxiety, then, is an emotion that signals to the Freudian the presence of some unconscious belief or fear. From that point of view, anxiety has an important function: it keeps us from becoming conscious of our unconscious beliefs, for we tend to avoid feeling anxiety. Since these beliefs are unconscious precisely because we, in some sense, don't wish to become aware of them, anxiety functions as an alarm that warns us not to think about such things. Only in the context of therapy, can we confront our anxieties and discover their unconscious causes.

The Existentialists, especially Sartre, were hostile to such Freudian explanations. There are many reasons for this. Most generally, they tended to frown on the use that Sigmund Freud (1856–1939) and his followers made of unconscious mental states. Instead, they thought that our mental life is more transparent to us than the Freudians maintained. In addition, they objected to the postulation of agencies within the mind – such as the 'censor.' So, in the example above, they would reject the idea that there was a part of a person that did not want the unconscious belief to become conscious. Such subpersonal agency just did not make sense to them. But in the case of anxiety, there is a more specific reason why the Existentialists reject the Freudian explanation of it: they see something much more significant as its cause. Like the Freudians, they think that our anxiety conceals something from our view, keeps us away from a troubling truth. But, unlike the Freudians, they think that it is an unpleasant *metaphysical* truth that our anxiety helps us avoid.

Although the Existentialists all emphasized the significance that anxiety has in our lives, they gave very different accounts of it. Here, I will follow Sartre's analysis of it. In chapter 7, I will return to the subject of anxiety in connection with Heidegger's analysis of death.

To help us understand the alternative viewpoint that the Existentialists have about the object of anxiety, let's think about the experience that Robert Frost captures in his well-known and often anthologized poem, 'The Road Not Taken.' The narrator of the poem comes across two paths in the forest and has to decide which one to take. He looks at one and thinks that it's just fine, but then chooses the other because, he says, it appears to be 'less traveled.' Although he initially presents this as the reason for his choice, he quickly admits that the path he chose was actually no less worn. He tells us that the first path really appeared 'just as fair' as the second, so a supposed difference in the conditions of the paths can't really justify his choice between the equally well-trodden ways. Nonetheless, at the end of the poem, he imagines describing his decision at some indeterminate point in the future in the very terms he has just admitted are not adequate to explain his decision: 'I took the one less traveled by,/And that has made all the difference.' This strikes an attentive reader as odd, for the narrator has already admitted the inadequacy of that explanation. So his sense of himself as a nonconformist who takes the less worn paths in life is inaccurate. Nothing in his life can be attributed to his choosing to take the nonconformist option, for the two paths that Frost uses as a metaphor for choosing how to live one's life were, by the narrator's own admission, equally well traveled. This poem has a narrator who accepts a way of thinking about decision-making that he knows not to be true but adopts nonetheless because it allows him to have a self-image he likes. He accepts a rationale to justify his choice that he knows to be false, because it allows him to see himself as a nonconformist who doesn't follow the common way. Frost's poem is thus an excellent example of Bad Faith.

But although 'The Road Not Taken' is about self-deception, I want to consider a different aspect of it here: its depiction of a situation in which a person must make a choice that he takes to be a fundamental one in his life. After all, that is exactly how the narrator imagines his situation: he thinks he is facing a choice that will make 'all the difference.' Although he does not express any anxiety over having to make this choice, his situation is one that can, and often does, result in anxiety. I think here of my having to decide which of two jobs I would take after finishing my graduate studies. I was interviewed at a number of universities and offered positions at two of them. I knew that this was an all-important decision, for the rest of my life would be affected by the choice that I made between these two jobs. I imagined, correctly I think, that what I decided would impact virtually every aspect of my life: who my friends would be; how my career would go; who I would marry, if anyone; and so on. But I couldn't figure out which choice was the right one or even how to go about preparing to make the decision. Unlike the simple decisions of life – such as what to eat for breakfast – there didn't seem to be any information that was available that could help me make a rational choice. As a result, simply having to make this decision caused me deep anxiety. I vacillated for a long time, talked to many friends, all in hopes of finding that one of the two jobs would be my 'road less traveled by,' but to no avail. Finally, I just had to go with what I can only describe as a gut feeling, a sense that one of the two universities was a better fit for me, although I couldn't really explain why that was. I had no good rationale that I could point to as justifying my decision.

What was the source of my anxiety about which job to take? Nothing but the fact of having to make a decision and my recognition that my life, the only one I have to live, would be fundamentally shaped by my decision in ways that I could not anticipate. Although I could not find a rational approach for making the decision, I still had to make it. Most of the time, when we have to make decisions in our life, we can point to something that justifies our choice. When I look at a menu in a restaurant and decide on what dish to order, for example, I can usually provide an explanation for my choice by citing my passion for wild mushrooms, say. Of course, I can make mistakes and be disappointed, but my decision-making is still a rational process in which I have good reasons for my decision. But this was not how my situation appeared in the case of the two jobs, for there was no way to accurately anticipate what either alternative would be like. How could I decide which job to accept when I knew that what I decided would fundamentally alter my future but I had no way of imagining how? All that I could feel about having to make this decision was *Angst*, the Existentialists' favorite term for anxiety!

If this situation is typical of the major decisions that we have to make in our lives, what answer does it suggest to the question of what anxiety is *about*? It may come as a surprise, but the Existentialists' answer is that anxiety is about a fundamental fact about what it is to be human: its 'object' is the fact that we have to make decisions that 'make all the difference,' but have nothing to rely on in making them. Anxiety is a reflection of this aspect of our situation. This is one feature of our *finitude* as human beings, a fact about our lives that the Existentialists thought had not been sufficiently acknowledged by previous philosophers: that we lack adequate grounds for deciding the fundamental issues of our lives.

Although I will defer a more complete discussion of human finitude and the role it plays in Existentialism to the next chapter, I do want to consider why the Existentialists thought that previous philosophers had not completely integrated the fact of our finitude into their accounts of our nature as humans. A good place to begin is with the idea of the *leap of faith* as developed by Søren Kierkegaard (see text box opposite).

The Danish philosopher **Søren Kierkegaard** (1813–1855) was the father of Existentialism. Kierkegaard developed his philosophy in opposition to two things. First, he opposed Hegel's philosophical approach for its insistence that human beings ascend to a universal point of view. In place of this, he emphasized the fundamental importance of *individuality*, a key theme for later Existentialist philosophers. Second, he rejected the Danish Church for its emphasis upon the sacraments as the measure of religious faith. Kierkegaard advocated the inner nature of faith rather than its outer display. For him, the behavior of the person of faith was indistinguishable from that of anyone else. Still, Kierkegaard emphasized the difficulty of attaining faith, for it was based upon beliefs that appear to have no basis in ordinary human experience.

Kierkegaard wrote most of his major philosophical works pseudonymously. These include *Either/Or: A Fragment of Life*, 'edited' by Victor Eremita (1843), *Fear and Trembling: A Dialectical Lyric*, by Johannes de Silentio (1843), *Philosophical Fragments: Or a Fragment of Philosophy*, by Johannes Climacus (1844), and *Concluding Unscientific Postscript to Philosophical Fragments* (1846), also by Climacus.

Kierkegaard's philosophical theories deeply reflected the course of his life. His writings included, in veiled form, reflections on the various life-crises he faced, including an abortive love affair, which became a source for many of his philosophical reflections on the nature of faith.

The leap of faith

Kierkegaard developed the notion of the leap of faith in presenting his answer to the question of whether God exists. One of the interesting features of Existentialism is that it is broad enough to encompass determined atheists such as Sartre as well as avowed theists (believers in God) such as Kierkegaard, even if the theism of the Existentialists is not the traditional kind. What's distinctive about Kierkegaard's theism – and what makes it so similar to Sartre's atheism as a philosophical view – is its rejection of a rational basis for faith in the existence of God and its emphasis upon a person's individuality through her relationship to God.

One of the basic tasks of traditional metaphysics was proving or disproving the existence of God. After all, metaphysics was the philosophical discipline whose goal was explaining the nature of all existence, and God is certainly one of the most important entities whose existence is subject to question. (Numbers and universals are examples of two other types of things whose existence some metaphysicians doubted. Philosophers who deny the existence of these abstract entities are called 'nominalists.') As a result, there are a number of different routes by which philosophers have sought to prove God's existence. Perhaps the most famous, developed by St Anselm of Canterbury (1033–1109), is the *ontological proof*. The lynch pin of this proof is its contention that the concept of God is of such an amazing and complete being that his existence follows simply from the nature of the concept itself. Here is a quick sketch of the proof. If we think of God as the greatest of all possible beings, then he must exist, because, if not, we can think of a being greater than God, namely the being who shares all of God's attributes plus that of existence. But God is the greatest of all *possible*, not just actual, beings, so that other being cannot be greater than God and this means that God must necessarily exist. QED as philosophers say; it has been demonstrated.

Many react to the ontological proof of God's existence just as they do to a magician's pulling a rabbit out of his hat. They are convinced there must be some gimmick that accounts for the trick working. Others are not convinced that the trick actually works at all! Still, over the centuries, many philosophers thought it was convincing. So even Descartes, who initiated modern Western philosophy by supposedly doubting all that could be doubted, cast his lot in with the ontological proof. Although the proof was criticized by the empiricist philosopher David Hume, only when Immanuel Kant claimed that there was a logical flaw in it in *The Critique of Pure Reason* (1781), did it lose its credibility within the Western tradition. (Kant questioned the traditional understanding of existence as a property like *being red* or *having hair.*)

Kierkegaard's development of the idea of the leap of faith is, at least in part, a reaction to Kant's discrediting the traditional proofs of God's existence, including the ontological proof. Rather than attempting to show that there was a new and improved proof that was not liable to Kant's criticism, as many lesser philosophers attempted in the face of Kant's skeptical attack, Kierkegaard admitted that Kant was right. From the point of view of ordinary human experience, there is no way to *prove* that God exists. But rather than being defeated in his *belief* in God by this, Kierkegaard merely responded: So much the worse for *proofs*. God's existence is a matter of *faith*. In order to have faith, you cannot rely on rational proof. You have to take a leap and stake your entire existence on your faith. (Kierkegaard's idea that one had to stake one's *existence* on what one had faith in is one origin of the term '*Existence*-ialism.')

Kierkegaard's manner of supporting his philosophical position involved many unusual writing styles, including the use of pseudonyms and the creation of narrative personas who do not share his own outlook. But in his writings, Kierkegaard also presents a number of important examples of people who exhibited the nature of faith as he conceived it. He calls such exemplary individuals 'knights of faith' and one of his prime examples of such a knight comes from the Old Testament; Abraham, the father of the Judeo–Christian–Islamic tradition. Kierkegaard asks us to think about Abraham's situation when God asked him to sacrifice his son, Isaac. Although God had promised Abraham in the original covenant he made with him that Abraham would be the father of a great nation, for many years Abraham was unable to have a child with his wife, Sarah. In fact, Isaac's birth was a miracle because of the advanced age of his parents. So when God asks Abraham to take his miraculously produced son, Isaac, and sacrifice him upon Mount Moriah, it should have been a real shock to Abraham. First, God gives Abraham a son in a miracle and then he tells him that he has to kill him! How can God keep his covenant without Abraham having a son from whom the great nation of Israel could descend? Why the very idea is *absurd*! Doesn't Abraham have to have a son in order to be the father of a great nation, as God promised? Yet God now demands that Abraham sacrifice the very son who must be alive for God's promise to be fulfilled. That just doesn't make sense. And, of all the things he could ask of Abraham, God tells him to do the one that is probably most abhorrent to any parent: kill his own beloved offspring. Is God a sadist?

How does Abraham react to God's apparently cruel and irrational order? Instead of questioning God and asking him why he requires this abhorrent sacrifice, he simply does what God asks:

> And Abraham rose up early in the morning, and saddled his ass, and two of his young men with him, and Isaac his son, and clave the wood for the burnt offering, and rose up, and went unto the place of which God had told him. (Genesis 22:3)

Amazing! No *Angst*! No recriminations against God! Abraham acts as if God had told him to go to the store for a cup of coffee, not to sacrifice his son. Abraham plays the part of a dutiful servant and sets off to do exactly what God asked of him without a moment's hesitation. How could he manage this?

Kierkegaard pushes us to see the absurdity of Abraham's faith because he takes such absurdity to be characteristic of faith in general. To have faith in God is to believe in the absurd, that which is contrary to the standards of everyday human reason. So Kierkegaard's answer is that Abraham is able to do what God asks without any apparent hesitation because he believes in the absurd, something that is beyond the power of human reason to comprehend. Abraham must believe two contradictory propositions: that his son Isaac shall found a great nation and that he needs to sacrifice Isaac as God asks. From our ordinary point of view, there is a contradiction between these two statements, so both of them can't be true. But *the absurd* is precisely that which flouts the conventions of human rationality. Abraham's acceptance of the absurd – the basis of all faith, according to Kierkegaard – allows him to do as God asks.

Although this example is drawn from the Old Testament, Kierkegaard is thinking generally about Christianity in his discussion of faith and the absurd. And there are many features of Christianity that exemplify these notions. For example, traditional Christian doctrine says that God is three distinct entities at once: the Father, the Son, and the Holy Ghost. It is a basic principle of logic, however, that any thing can only be identical with itself, so that all things that are identical to each other are the same. Thus, to understand God as three distinct, coexisting things is to countenance an absurdity, something that is an affront to human reason! But rather than being dismayed by this contention and trying to find a way to explain Christian belief in a way that makes it harmonize with human rationality, Kierkegaard says, in effect, 'Exactly! Faith requires us to accept the absurd, that which violates the norms of human reason.'

Kierkegaard points out that there are many other features of traditional religion that appear absurd from the point of view of common sense. According to Judaism, God is not visible, yet Moses was able to talk with him when he appeared in the guise of a burning bush. How much sense does that make from our everyday point of view? And what about an immaterial God deciding to take on human form, as the Christian God is supposed to have? Does that make any more sense from a strictly empirical point of view? Think about how we would now feel if we ran into somebody who claimed that God had appeared to him in the form of a burning bush or, worse yet, someone who claimed to be the daughter of God. Most of us would be much more likely, I think, to send her to a psychiatrist than to believe that what she said was true. And at least part of the reason for this is that we think that the standards we use to assess our everyday experience are the right ones for distinguishing what's real from what's not. But it is just these standards that Kierkegaard insists have to be jettisoned to have faith.

But why does Kierkegaard claim that faith requires a *leap*? First, he believes all of us start out accepting the idea that the principles we use to make sense of our everyday experience are the best guides to what's real. This is a pretty normal assumption. As we try to make sense of the world, we rely on principles that work in that context. We learn, for example, that not everything that appears to our senses is real, that there are things like rainbows and hallucinations whose being has to be distinguished from the being of things like tables and chairs. So we claim that such things are merely *apparent*. We call the principles that we use to make such determinations those of *common sense*, and they become the standards for judging what is reasonable.

But what if there really are things that we cannot understand so long as we accept only these principles derived from our normal, everyday experience? (In addition to thinking about God, you can think of the ghost of Hamlet's father and Hamlet's famous rejoinder to the skeptical Horatio, 'There are more things in heaven and earth, Horatio,/Than are dreamt of in your philosophy' (*Hamlet* I, v, 165–6).) It would be circular to assert that such things *cannot exist* because our common sense principles do not recognize them, for these principles by their very nature cannot reach such un-common things. In such a case, our everyday standards and those required for making judgments about what we might call *super-sensible* reality would be *incommensurable*. There would be no common standard that we could use to judge the two types of realities.

Kierkegaard maintains that our ordinary world of rational common sense and the irrational world of religious faith are incommensurable in just this sense. From our everyday perspective, the world of faith appears *absurd*, quite literally contrary to the rational standards we use to make determinations about the objects in our experience. The existence of a Man-God is absurd from the point of view of our everyday experience, but that does not mean such a thing cannot exist, only that its existence would require that we drop the point of view of common sense and entertain that of religion or faith. From *that* point of view – as we can tell from the testimony of those who embrace it – it is just as one-sided to believe only in the existence of temporal things. The two points of view cannot be reconciled: they are incommensurable. But this does not mean that either has the right to deny the validity of the other.

So if one is to deny the adequacy of the everyday perspective and embrace faith, one must reject the standards employed within the former. This is the reason that Kierkegaard says that we have to make a *leap* in order to attain faith. The world of faith has completely different standards from those of the everyday world of common sense, so one cannot move to it from the everyday in some gradual transition, as one does, for example, in traveling to New York City when one first encounters the suburbs and then slowly encounters more dense areas of population until one arrives at the skyscraper-dominated island of Manhattan. The two realms of the ordinary and of faith are so different from each other that there can be no gradual transition from one to the other. So Kierkegaard analogizes the situation to standing on the edge of a precipice over which you must *leap* to get to the other side.

But now consider the question of whether you ought to accept the religious point of view. Clearly, to do so would be a momentous decision, for you would be accepting a point of view for which you had no rational basis. Yet, it is the sort of decision that, in the words of the narrator of Frost's poem, makes all the difference. So, how can you decide what to do?

Here is where the notion of anxiety comes into play in Kierkegaard's account of the leap of faith. The person who faces the decision of whether to accept religion will surely experience a great deal of anxiety because so much hangs on that decision and there is no reliable, noncontroversial evidence upon which to base it. One will have to make that decision in *fear and trembling*, as Kierkegaard says, referring to Philippians chapter 2, verse 12. The reason is that one will have to leave the world of ordinary human experience to base one's life on a principle for which one has none of the usual evidence we rely on in making decisions.

So Kierkegaard agrees with Sartre that anxiety signals an important fact about human life: that we have to make crucial decisions without having a standard to appeal to in making them. Unlike the decision made by Frost's narrator, it is really true that everything in our lives hangs on what we decide about such fundamental matters as the existence of God, but it's also true that, in making such decisions, there is no 'evidence' that we can use to justify our decision. For many things in life, even important ones, we can find reasons that explain and justify what we have done. A friend of mine told me recently, for example, that he had finally decided to quit smoking because he decided that the health dangers it posed were simply too great. In this case, he had a rational basis for his decision, something that he could refer to in order to explain it to me and that was a perfectly adequate justification of it. But Kierkegaard's contention is that, in the most fundamental decision of our life – whether to believe in God – there is nothing that we can use to justify our decision in a way that others will understand. We must decide, but we can't rationally justify or explain our decision. Hence, the incredible anxiety we face about such a momentous decision that has to be made without having the usual reasons to support it — at least those of us who are not knights of faith like Abraham. How could we abandon our common sense worldview and accept the existence of things beyond our senses and not be consumed with anxiety?

Although Kierkegaard develops his idea of the leap of faith in the context of explaining the nature of the religious worldview, the account of human decision-making he gives has wider applicability. Indeed, in the second chapter we saw that the atheistic Existentialist philosopher Sartre treats all decision-making as structurally similar to deciding whether to believe in God. Sartre and other atheistic Existentialists accepted Kierkegaard's analysis of anxiety and decision-making but rejected religious faith as the central context within which we experience it. For Sartre, we experience anxiety because we lack rational justifications for all the crucial decisions in our lives.

Encountering ourselves

We are now finally ready to resolve the puzzle about anxiety that I raised at the beginning of this chapter: that it seems not to have any object and thus appears to contradict the thesis of the intentionality of mental states. According to the Existentialist analysis of anxiety, the object of that crucial emotion is nothing but ourselves or, as Sartre might say, the nothing that is ourselves. (See, speaking that way can be fun!) For the most part, we humans simply avoid anxiety — and the Existentialists spend a great deal of effort in revealing all of the highly creative forms that we have invented to do so, as we shall continue to explore in subsequent chapters. But through the use of the phenomenological method, we can discover that *we ourselves* are the object of our anxiety, because we have the freedom to make decisions about how to live our lives, indeed, we are, as Sartre puts it, *condemned* to be free. Since we have no rational grounds for making the fundamental decisions we must as free beings, anxiety is simply our way of registering in the depths of our being our difficult and upsetting situation.

Thus, anxiety provides the key experience for acquiring an understanding of our nature, according to the Existentialists. Because our first experience of ourselves is through the eyes of others, we initially have a distorted view of what we are. Facing our own anxiety allows us to attain a more accurate view of our own nature. Unlike many other emotions, anxiety has a deep metaphysical significance: it brings into our experience a true understanding of what the nature of human existence is really like.

Let me end this chapter by emphasizing that the Existentialist analysis of anxiety is an excellent example of the *phenomenological method* that the Existentialists follow and think is the correct way to do philosophy. Accordingly, the abstract analysis put forward about the nature of any phenomenon that we want to understand philosophically has to be confirmed through an analysis of an actual human experience. In this respect, the Existentialists differ from other schools of philosophy that only put forward their own theories without attempting to confirm them experientially. Because the Existentialists employ a version of the phenomenological method, they always trace their abstract philosophical claims – 'life is absurd,' 'anxiety reveals the nature of our existence' – back to very specific human experiences. This is part of why so many people find this form of philosophizing so compelling, for it starts with our ordinary experience as human beings and shows it to have deep, philosophical significance.

5

Finitude

In the last chapter, I noted that the Existentialists thought previous philosophers had not taken seriously enough the fact of our *finitude* as human beings. On the face of it, this seems an odd claim, for no one can seriously doubt that human beings are finite creatures. There are, after all, many ways in which we are limited. We all have to die, even though we do not know when; we all have limitations in what we can do, though our aspirations often outstrip our abilities; and our knowledge is also limited, so that we often act in ignorance, a fact made a great deal of by, among others, the Greek tragedians. In our life span, our abilities, our knowledge, and our actions, humans are undeniably finite. So how could philosophers have failed to acknowledge this?

The answer begins with God, for he is conceived within the Judeo–Christian–Islamic tradition to be in a very different position than we are. In every way that humans are limited, God is unlimited. Hence, his description as eternal, all-knowing, all-powerful, and all-good. One way to grasp our finitude – and many people's dissatisfaction with it – is to see it in relation to our notion of a perfect being who does not participate in our infirmities, who possesses all that we lack.

There seem to be two basic philosophical strategies for dealing with the undeniable fact that we are finite creatures. The first, tracing its roots all the way back to the Greek philosopher Plato (429–347 BCE), is to try to overcome it as best we can. Since Plato conceived of humans as having aspects of the divine within them, he thought human life ought to aim at validating our divine aspects, so that they could rule over (and overrule) our finite features. This *rationalist tradition* taught that humans ought to live so as to overcome their limitations as finite beings and aspire to instantiate a divine, and hence complete, being, most notably by denying our desires in favor of the demands of reason.

Plato's pupil Aristotle began the alternative philosophical tradition of *empiricism*. For the empiricist, it was a mistake to try to overcome our finitude. Instead, the philosophical project of empiricism was to explicate the nature of *human* knowing, doing, and valuing, not what such capacities might be like in a being fundamentally different from us. Rather than aspiring to root out that in which we differ from the divine, the empiricists acknowledged our finitude and its effect on every aspect of our being. This is not to say that Aristotle was a completely consistent empiricist. Despite his concern to do justice to human experience, like his teacher Plato, he suggested that humans should seek to realize what was most god-like in themselves in his account of what is best for humans in *The Nichomachean Ethics*. Nonetheless, he paved the way for subsequent empiricist concern with acknowledging human finitude.

In this respect, Existentialism belongs to the empiricist camp, for it emphasizes how the fact of our finitude affects every aspect of our lives: our knowing, our acting, and our valuing – the three activities philosophers had taken to be adequate to characterize human life. Indeed, Existentialism can even be thought of as a form of *radical empiricism*, to borrow a phrase from William James, because the Existentialists attempted to root out all traces of the rationalist model of philosophy. They believed that, in Nietzsche's apt phrase, we were 'human, all too human,' so that it was an error to think of ourselves as simply limited versions of an infinite being. They took our finitude to be an ineliminable part of our nature, so that our philosophical account of ourselves ought to reflect its pervasiveness.

A good place to begin our investigation of how the Existentialists developed a more adequate account of human finitude is with a problem that faced the Judeo–Christian account of religious belief: the problem of evil. One of the traditional obstacles facing theists is the existence of evil, the fact that terrible events occur. It has always been hard for any observer of human affairs to deny the horrors of human life. Natural disasters routinely kill many people and human-inflicted misery has pervaded our history. Philosophers have conceived of these events as 'evils,' bad things that befall human beings. The problem that evils pose for the theist is to explain how God could let them happen. It is sometimes asserted that the existence of evil shows that God is either malicious or incompetent. But within the Judeo–Christian tradition, God is conceived of as omniscient, omnipotent, and beneficent: all-knowing, all-powerful, and supremely good. So the question facing the theist is to explain how such a supreme being could allow evil – both physical (natural) and moral (caused by people) – to exist and, even, appear to flourish. The problem of evil, as these philosophical considerations are generally labeled, dates all the way back to the Greek philosopher Epicurus (341–270 BCE), who used it to justify his atheism.

The philosopher who did the most to defend theism proper in the face of the argument from evil was the German rationalist philosopher Gottfried Wilhelm Leibniz (see text box overleaf). Leibniz took seriously the challenge that the existence of evil posed for the theist and put forward one of the most startling defenses imaginable: that this is, in fact, the best of all possible worlds. On the face of it, this contention seems absurd. There is simply too much pain and suffering in life to justify claiming this to be the best of all possible worlds. Only a blind optimist could be capable of denying that human life is full of horrors. The names Hitler, Stalin, Hiroshima, Nagasaki, Mao, and Pol Pot just begin to indicate the terrible course of events in the twentieth century alone. How could one possibly maintain the optimistic thesis put forward by Leibniz in the face of such tragically compelling evidence? (There were terrible events before the twentieth century that caused many to reject Leibniz's view. The Lisbon earthquake of 1755, for example, resulted in Voltaire's stinging satire of Leibniz's view, *Candide*.)

Gottfried Wilhelm Leibniz (1646–1716) was a polymath, inventing calculus and conducting world affairs as an advisor for the House of Hanover while also writing metaphysical treatises. Perhaps because of his busy life, Leibniz tended to write essays, many of which were published only posthumously, rather than the lengthier tomes favored by his contemporaries.

Leibniz's central metaphysical thesis was that the world consists of an infinite number of simple entities or 'monads.' Each monad was self-contained yet reflected the entire nature of the world in a way that depended upon its state of perfection, with the more perfect monads having a clearer perception of reality. On the basis of this metaphysics, Leibniz attempted to solve many traditional puzzles of Western philosophy. Because Leibniz denied that relationships between things were real, his idealist philosophy avoided many traditional problems such as that of the interaction between mind and body.

The *Theodicy* (1709), Leibniz's last published work, was an extended attempt to justify his solution to the problem of evil. His ideas attained great popularity in Germany after his death, when they became more or less the official philosophy of the age.

The prevalence of pain and suffering in our lives, and throughout the world in general, puts an incredible burden of proof on one who wishes to maintain that this is the best of all possible worlds. How, in the face of so much empirical evidence against his thesis, could Leibniz have seriously maintained it?

The lynch pin of Leibniz's defense of his view is the notion of *compossibility*. To call a number of distinct things *compossible* is to assert not only that each one is possible on its own, but also that all of the individual things are *jointly* possible. So, for example, it is possible that an oak tree was planted directly in front of my house. It is also possible that a maple tree was planted there. But it is not possible that both an oak tree and a maple tree be directly in front of my house, since two things cannot be in the same place at the same time. So even though two things are both possible, they may not be *compossible*; there might not be a possible world in which both can exist.

How does the notion of compossibility provide a solution to the problem of evil? Leibniz admitted that it certainly looked like God simply let many awful things occur. But rather than saying that this showed God to be malevolent or incompetent, Leibniz argued that God had actually created a world that contained as much good as it was possible to include. The reason why we think he has created a less than perfect world, according to Leibniz, is that we persist in viewing it from only our own small corner of the universe. Sure, if your best friend is dying of a painful and debilitating progressive illness, you think God certainly could have made a better world than this one. But that's only *your* own point of view on things as a finite individual. What Leibniz asked us to acknowledge is that, if we consider all the individuals in the universe *taken together*, then this very world must be the best of all possible worlds that God could have created because it allows for the greatest amount of well-being for each individual that is possible along with the maximum amount of well-being for all the other individuals in the world. The key idea is that not everything that appears to us to be possible from our limited perspective as finite beings is really possible, for knowledge of real possibility requires putting a given 'possibility' together with everything else that makes up the world. Sure, it would be nice if your friend did not have a terrible disease. But if God had spared your friend, then another – *worse* – consequence would have had to exist somewhere else in the universe, such as, perhaps, an awful genocide. Because he is able to consider all the possible worlds that could have existed,

God creates the world that incorporates the greatest amount of good that is actually possible, even though this entails that the actual world must include so much pain and suffering.

An interesting feature of Leibniz's account of the world is his conception of God's decision-making process in creating the universe. God began by thinking about all the possible worlds that there were. From what we've already discussed, it's clear that God had to consider not just the existence of each thing that could populate a given world, but how it would mesh with all the other things that might exist in that world. This is the whole import of Leibniz's notion of compossibility, as we saw in the example of the two trees in front of my home. Figuring out what things are compossible is a daunting task. God would have to think about each existing thing, understand everything that would happen to it in the course of its existence – no mean feat – build up possible worlds from knowledge of their constituents, and compare each of those possible worlds with one another. Fortunately, God, as Leibniz conceived him, was not just infinitely good; because his knowledge was infinite, he could just trot out all of this information with ease. In each case of thinking about a possible world, he would not only have to think about everything that would happen in the history of that world, but he would also have to calculate the amount of goodness that each world contains. In the end, he chose to create this world, the one that we inhabit, because it contains the greatest amount of goodness possible in a world.

As I have said, given the amount of pain and suffering that exists in our world, it is hard to accept Leibniz's claim that this is the best of all possible worlds. However, Leibniz believed that our inability to comprehend how this could be the best of all possible worlds did not mean that it is not. So, to defend his point of view, Leibniz developed a number of different metaphors and analogies. My favorite involves a landscape painting. Leibniz argued that a painting made up solely of beautiful colors will not be as beautiful as one that consists of both beautiful and ugly ones. For the sake of argument and for simplicity, let's accept the dubious hypothesis that black and brown are ugly colors and red, blue, and yellow beautiful ones. To protest that a painting should not have any black in it because black is an 'ugly' color is to fail to see that the beauty of a painting is created through the harmony of different colors working together, so that 'ugly' colors have a role to play in the creation of beauty. Leibniz thought we should think of evil as like an 'ugly' color: although we might object to its presence when we consider it by itself, by seeing its role in the overall pattern of things and their relationships, we could come to see why it had to exist.

It's hard for us, living in the twenty-first century, to realize how persuasive Leibniz's account was for his contemporaries. Still, his logic remains difficult to criticize and his analogies help to make his view plausible. Leibniz appeared to have saved an imperiled God from the pincers of the logical perplexity contained in the problem of evil. Particularly for theists, this was a welcome outcome!

The human perspective

From an Existentialist point of view, however, Leibniz's theory was fundamentally misguided. We can see this if we turn, yet once more, to the writings of the great Russian novelist, Fyodor Dostoevsky. We have already met one of his most memorable characters, Ivan, the middle of the three Karamazov brothers. Given Ivan's exposé of the Catholic Church in the parable of the Grand Inquisitor, it is not surprising to find him taking on Leibniz's solution to the problem of evil as well. And just as Kierkegaard did not object to Kant's claim that God's existence cannot be proved, Ivan does not target Leibniz's attempt to show that God's existence is compatible with the existence of evil. Rather, Ivan asserts that he simply refuses to accept the world if its existence requires that innocent people suffer.

To make his point, Ivan focuses on young, innocent children. This is important, for their suffering could then not be justified as retribution for evils that they have themselves committed, as might be the case with adults. The question Ivan asks is whether the suffering of such children can be resolved, as Leibniz claimed, in a 'higher harmony.' Ivan's denial is reinforced by a series of vignettes he tells in which innocent children are made to suffer abominably by their parents, by a cruel landowner, and so on. What Ivan refuses to concede is that somehow, there is a logic that can make *him* accept the reasonableness of such suffering.

> And if the suffering of children goes to make up the sum of suffering needed to buy truth, then I assert beforehand that the whole truth is not worth such a price ... I don't want harmony, for love of mankind I don't want it. I want to remain with unrequited suffering. I'd rather remain with my unrequited suffering and my unquenched indignation, *even if I am wrong*. Besides, they have put too high a price on harmony; we can't afford to pay so much for admission. And therefore I hasten to return my ticket ... It's not that I don't accept God, Alyosha, I just most respectfully return him the ticket. (*Brothers Karamazov*, 245)

Ivan does not attempt to show that there is a logical flaw in the Leibnizian argument that all suffering, even the terrible indignations suffered by innocent children, is necessary because of the role it plays in the creation of the whole of existence. Instead, he claims that he won't *accept* the terms on which such a view of the world is predicated. Even if this world is better than any other, that's not good enough for Ivan.

Ivan's criticism rejects the appeal Leibnizians make to divine rationality in order to justify the existence of evil. Ivan recognizes that Leibniz's argument will only work on the basis of his model of what God's decision-making must be like. Leibniz asks us, at least implicitly, to accept God's conclusions because his decision-making procedure is vastly superior to ours. Because God has superior knowledge to us, we are to reject our own human reaction to the suffering of innocent children: that it is absolutely evil. To call something an *absolute* evil is to say that it is so horrible it cannot be redeemed or justified in relation to something else. An example of an evil that can be redeemed − a relative evil − is the death of civilians in a just war (assuming that there is such a thing). We might admit that, even in war, civilian deaths are an evil, but argue that they are an unavoidable consequence of waging a just war, a war that, like World War II for many of us, we accept as having been necessary. But Ivan claims there are some evils that are so terrible *from his perspective as a human being* that they simply cannot be justified. The Leibnizian might respond by citing the notion of relative evil, and arguing that even the suffering of innocent children is redeemable since it is a necessary price we have to pay for the existence of the world and all the good that it brings with it. But Ivan simply refuses to play the game: he won't accept this world − view its existence as rational and justified − if the condition of its existence is the suffering of innocents. His dramatic gesture of handing God back the ticket of admission to this world means that he is willing to sacrifice even his own life in order to uphold his human perspective on suffering.

It's important to understand what the stakes are, from Ivan's point of view. He is affirming his own finite, human point of view over and against the divine one. He finds himself unable to take the divine point of view despite what the cost to himself might be, because he sees that adopting that point of view will force him to reject his important, all-too-human commitment to the assertion that the suffering of an innocent being is absolutely evil. Ivan has the audacity to affirm the validity of his own human perspective over and against God's.

This affirmation of the human over the divine is significant because the rationalist tradition of Western thought had endorsed the superiority of the divine perspective. It claimed that the divine perspective outstrips the human one because only it is true. From this point of view, God sees things as they really are, not simply as they appear to human beings, so we human beings should aspire to take his perspective on our own lives and the world as a whole. Indeed, it is not just the rationalist school of philosophy that urges us to accept this perspective, but most of the world's religions. From their standpoint, it is almost self-evident that we should prefer a more objective viewpoint to the one that we have as the limited beings that we are.

But Ivan urges that the adoption of a supposedly more complete, fuller, less limited take on things actually amounts to a denial of our own humanity. To be a human being is to be limited, finite, partial, incomplete. Our task is not to reject our own perspective as flawed and seek to somehow realize an approximation to the divine one, but rather to inhabit our own perspective as fully as we can.

In making this point, Ivan is completing a philosophical revolution that began with Immanuel Kant (see text box opposite). In *The Critique of Pure Reason*, Kant had argued that previous philosophers – by whom he meant rationalists in the Leibnizian mold – had developed a conception of knowledge that failed to take into account an important aspect of our nature as finite beings, namely, that our knowledge is tied to sense-perception (what he calls empirical 'intuition,' *Anschauung* in German). According to Kant, the Leibnizian view of knowledge relied too heavily on thinking that takes place in the absence of any empirical touchstone. To succeed in giving an adequate account of human knowledge, we had to admit that we cannot rid our picture of the world of the traces of our finitude, that we had to remain tied to our perceptual faculties. For this reason, he affirmed a need to place 'the possibility of experience' at the center of his own 'critical' metaphysics, for this would ensure that our picture of the world remained fully anchored in our humanity.

But whereas Kant denies the possibility of knowledge of a super-sensible object such as God, Ivan does not confront the theist theoretically. His concern is with the human world of pain and suffering. He brings his own human perspective to that realm by refusing to adopt the divine perspective according to which pain and suffering are the price that we have to pay for

Immanuel Kant (1724–1804) developed a philosophical system he called 'the Critical Philosophy.' Articulated in three great 'critiques' – *Critique of Pure Reason* (1781, second edition 1787), *The Critique of Practical Reason* (1788), and *Critique of Judgement* (1790) – the fundamental tenet of this system was that we can have knowledge only of things as they appear to us, 'phenomena.' Things as they really are, or 'noumena,' must forever lie outside of our theoretical grasp. But although we cannot have any knowledge of noumena, we are able to form beliefs about them and, indeed, it is necessary to do so in order to have a rational basis for ethics.

This bifurcated metaphysics allowed Kant to claim that he had solved all of the problems bequeathed to him by the Western tradition of metaphysics. Many of these stemmed from philosophers failing to acknowledge the distinction between phenomena and noumena, and therefore believing it was possible to have knowledge of the three crucial noumenal objects: God, the World, and the Self. Kant argued that we can have no a priori theoretical knowledge of any of them. The negative portion of the *Critique of Pure Reason* systematically destroyed the pretensions of previous philosophers to prove God's existence, to demonstrate the nature and extent of the World, and to establish the character of the self.

In his later years, Kant was so worried that he would not finish explicating the Critical Philosophy that he adhered to a rigid schedule. His walks around his native town of Königsberg were so regular that people were reportedly able to set their clocks by them.

the existence of our world. That view still retains vestiges of the biblical story of the Fall, for it affirms that merely existing as we do requires experiencing pain and suffering. Ivan affirms the horror of unjustified human suffering and rejects any viewpoint that seeks to deny its absolute significance.

Provocative as Ivan's argument is – and I still find it thrilling for its audacity – it is essentially a negative argument, claiming that we have to maintain our human perspective and rejecting the appeal to take a divine one. It needs to be supplemented by an account of what exactly the human perspective amounts to. One option is to go with Kant, for he clearly affirms the idea that our knowledge is inescapably marked by our finitude. But the Existentialists believed that Kant's humanization of metaphysics had to be radicalized. And it is just this radicalized metaphysics that we have explored in the first four chapters of this book, in which a portrait of the world and ourselves is painted not as these would appear from a divine perspective but as we actually experience them.

But if the complex metaphysics of the human manner of *being-in-the-world-alongside-others* that we have explored is a spelling out of the Existentialists' understanding of the implications of our finitude as humans, we have yet to explore a second aspect of their account of the finitude of human beings. They present an explanation of why this crucial feature of our nature has failed to be taken seriously by both philosophers and ordinary human beings in the course of their lives. And the crucial issue in this regard is the significance that our *deaths* have for us.

Although we all would admit that dying is part of what it is to be human, the Existentialists think that traditional philosophy has not provided an adequate account of the significance of this fact for the conduct of our lives. Consider, for example, Socrates' discussion of death in Plato's dialogue, *The Phaedo*. In this dialogue, Phaedo, a student of Socrates, tells Echecrates, another Ancient Greek philosopher, about Socrates' death. He reports that, shortly before he is scheduled to die for the offense of impiety, Socrates argued that death is not something that a real philosopher seeks to avoid:

> For I deem that the true disciple of philosophy is likely to be misunderstood by other men; they do not perceive that he is ever pursuing death and dying; and if this is true, why, having had the desire of death all his life long, should he repine at the arrival of that which he has been always pursuing and desiring? (*Phaedo*, 63e–64a)

The reason the philosopher 'pursues death' is that he realizes that having a body keeps him from gaining real knowledge. Since knowledge or wisdom is the goal of philosophy, Socrates says that death, which he regards as the separation of the soul from the body, is a good thing, for it enables a person – now a disembodied soul – to attain real knowledge. So death is not something that a philosopher should fear. And Socrates himself maintained great equanimity in the face of his own impending death, if Plato's account is to be trusted.

In the present context, we can see that Socrates' conception of philosophy and death is based upon a similar conception of the aspirations of humans to that operative in Leibniz, for the knowledge that Socrates takes to be the goal of philosophy cannot be acquired by human beings during their lifetime. Although a philosophical life can bring one as close as humanly possible to such knowledge, only being free of our bodies would let us really attain it. The desire for an immaterial existence is akin to the desire, evident in Leibniz, to see the world from the point of view of God, a pure intelligence.

It is quite typical for readers of *The Phaedo* to be impressed by the portrait it paints of Socrates. Most of us regard death as something to be feared, so Socrates' equanimity as he stares it in the face strikes us as admirable and something to which we might even aspire. His attitude acquires its patina from its distance from our ordinary understanding of death. But what exactly is *that*?

Fleeing from death

The Existentialist who spells out our 'average everyday' attitude toward death is Heidegger. The first thing that he emphasizes is that, although we all know, in one sense, that we are going to die, there is another sense in which we are not fully aware of that fact, for we don't allow it to affect how we live. In his story 'The Death of Ivan Ilych,' Leo Tolstoy (see text box opposite) illustrates this idea by exploring how his eponymous character exempted himself from the knowledge that he would die.

> The syllogism he had learnt from Kiezewetter's *Logic*: 'Caius is a man, men are mortal, therefore Caius is mortal,' had always seemed to him correct as applied to Caius, but certainly not as applied to himself. That Caius – man in the abstract – was mortal, was perfectly correct, but he was not Caius, not an abstract man, but a creature quite, quite separate from all others. ... 'If I had to die like Caius, I should have known it was so.'
> ('The Death of Ivan Ilych,' 131–2)

The narrator is referring here to a common syllogism that is still often used to teach logic. It begins with the general truth, 'All men are mortal.' Since 'Caius is a man,' this truth must apply to him, so that, using a basic principle of logic, one must conclude that 'Caius is mortal.' The narrator's remark that Ilych had failed to apply this to himself is very ironic, for there certainly is a sense in which Ilych knew he would die. Nonetheless, discovering that he has a fatal disease is a real shock to him. The question the narrator ironically poses is how this could be: how can we know that we are going to die and still be shocked to discover that we are dying?

Lev Nikolayevich Tolstoy (1828–1910), the great Russian writer, is probably best known for his realist novels – *War and Peace* (1865–1869) and *Anna Karenina* (1877). These two novels are among the greatest works of literature of all time and are unequaled in their scope and breadth. The former focuses on a group of young Russian aristocrats at the time of the Napoleonic Wars. Although it portrays them confronting fundamental issues about their lives as they mature during the years of the wars, the novel also contains lengthy philosophical ruminations by Tolstoy on the nature of history and the way in which it is distorted in the writings of historians. *Anna Karenina* is the tragic story of a woman's adulterous affair with a military man. It has been praised for its realism and its portrayal of the moral dilemmas surrounding sex, love, and marriage.

Tolstoy was also well known for many other types of writings, including plays, short stories, ethical treatises, and even an important work of philosophical aesthetics – *What is Art?* (1897). In each of these genres, he wrote masterpieces that are still the subject of both admiration and study. In addition to 'The Death of Ivan Ilych' (1886), 'The Kreutzer Sonata' (1889) is numbered among the greatest short stories ever written. And aestheticians still consider *What is Art?* to have made a unique contribution to our understanding of art.

At one level, the answer is obvious. While we are aware that we are going to die, we usually don't know *when*. As Heidegger points out, although our death is *certain* – that is, we all realize that we are finite mortal beings – its certainty is *indeterminate* – we don't know when we are going to die. Learning that we have a fatal disease makes our death more immediate in that we become aware that our death is impending, and this can account for our being shocked. As Heidegger says, 'death is understood as an indefinite something which, above all, must arrive from somewhere or other, but which is proximally *not yet present-at-hand* for oneself, and is therefore no threat' (*Being and Time*, 297).

Is this explanation for our shock at discovering that we have a fatal disease adequate? Not according to the Existentialists. What they emphasize is that humans often structure their lives as if they would live forever, thereby failing to incorporate the fact of mortality into their lives in any significant way. As Heidegger puts it, *Dasein flees* in the face of death (*Being and Time*, 298).

We find a variety of different ways in which people attempt to flee from the knowledge of their own deaths portrayed in 'The Death of Ivan Ilych.' The story begins in the law courts as Ivan Ilych's colleagues read the news of his death. Tolstoy describes a range of different responses, all of which are attempts to fend off the thought of one's own mortality. First, people think about how Ivan Ilych's death will affect their careers:

> So on receiving the news of Ivan Ilych's death the first thought of each of the gentlemen in that private room [in the law court] was of the changes and promotions it might occasion among themselves or their acquaintances. ('The Death of Ivan Ilych,' 96)

Tolstoy also describes the relief people feel because it was someone else, not they, who had died: 'The mere fact of the death of a near acquaintance aroused, as usual, in all who heard of it the complacent feeling that, "it is he who is dead and not I"' (96). At his funeral, Ivan Ilych's two best friends are more concerned about scheduling a card game than they are about his death. Even his widow seems to be thinking more about her pension than the fact that her husband has died.

One way to understand this odd state of affairs – the human denial of death – is by means of Heidegger's notion of a They. You'll recall that Heidegger claimed that, in our 'average everyday' experience of others, *the They* function to enforce social standards for appropriate behavior. Rather than thinking about what we might want, the 'tyranny' of the They forces us to think only about what 'one' does in certain circumstances. In fact, Tolstoy describes the behavior of Ivan Ilych's best friend at his funeral in precisely these terms:

> And Peter Ivanovich knew that, just as it had been the right thing to cross himself in that room [where Ivan Ilych's body is lying], so what he had to do here was to press her hand, sigh, and say, 'Believe me...' So he did all this and as he did it felt that the desired result had been achieved: that both he and she were touched. ('The Death of Ivan Ilych,' 99–100)

When described in this way, a person seems to be a marionette whose strings are controlled by the They. He acts in ways that are prescribed as 'the right thing to do' by the They and even feels what the They deems it appropriate for him to feel.

Even this quick look at Tolstoy's story provides an answer to a question that I posed at the end of chapter 3: why would a person conform to the demands of the They so completely? 'The Death of Ivan Ilych' suggests that we allow ourselves to become social conformists in order to keep at bay the knowledge of our own finitude, awareness of our own deaths. So, instead of focusing on all that makes him uncomfortable at Ivan Ilych's funeral, his friend Peter Ivanovich thinks about how he is supposed to behave, thereby keeping at bay such discomfiting reflections as 'The thought of the sufferings of this man he had known so intimately ... suddenly struck Peter Ivanovich with horror ... He again saw that brow, and that nose pressing down on the lip, and felt afraid for himself' (101–2). Here, Peter Ivanovich succumbs to an awareness of his own mortality. But for the most part, while in the presence of the body of his friend, he is able to fend off such 'morbid' thoughts by worrying about not appearing ill-mannered and by focusing on how inconvenient Ivan Ilych's death is, having thrown his plans for a card game into confusion. By keeping to his routines and focusing on proprieties, Peter Ivanovich manages, for the most part, to keep his friend's death from forcing him to realize that his own death is likewise an impending event.

Although these everyday strategies are important as ways of keeping knowledge of our own death at bay, there is a more obvious strategy that humans also use: denying the finality of death. When Socrates does that in *The Phaedo*, he claims that death is not the end of his existence, but only a *transformation* of it. Since he conceives of himself as having a soul that is entrapped in a body, he can view death as a liberation, for it frees that part of him he most values, his soul, from that which has kept it prisoner, his body. When looked at in this way, death is not something to be feared but embraced, as Socrates suggests, for it allows one to live without the encumbrance of having a body.

This Platonic conception of death is not limited to adherents of his own metaphysics of Forms. In fact, many of the world's religions, especially Christianity and Islam, accept something like it in their view of heaven and an afterlife. As a result, the Existentialists' critique of this way of thinking is extremely important and relevant. From their point of view, this attitude toward death is deeply flawed. Among the features of it to which they object is its dependence on a dualistic conception of the human being. Since one of the fundamental tenets of Existentialism is that the human being is an essentially embodied being, they think that it is a mistake to see oneself as a soul entrapped in a body. As a result, the idea of death as a liberation is fundamentally misguided. As we shall see, from the Existentialist point of view, death is final, an end to the being of the human being. And in affirming the finality of death over and against a view of death as a liberation into a more God-like existence, the Existentialists refuse to transcend one of the features of our lives – our deaths – that most firmly establishes us as the finite creatures that we are.

6
The Absurd

While discussing Kierkegaard's notion of the leap of faith a couple of chapters back, I introduced without much comment a term that many people associate with Existentialism: the absurd. Kierkegaard claimed that the basic feature of religion was its positing of things that were *absurd*, that is, contrary to reason. The number of such beliefs at the heart of Christianity, to choose one prominent example, is manifold: a virgin birth, an infinite God that takes on human form, a death that leads to a resurrection, and so on. Kierkegaard asked people to take seriously the fact that Judeo–Christian religious beliefs defy common sense and human rationality not in order to convince them to reject those beliefs, but rather to get people to see exactly what having faith involves and why, as a result, it is so difficult for human beings to attain. Indeed, some of the most famous narrators of his works marvel at the ability of people such as Abraham to act on the basis of their 'absurd' religious beliefs. Notice that calling a religious belief 'absurd' is not a way of denigrating it, but a matter of describing a specific feature of it: its violation of the norms of human reason.

So it is important to realize that the Existentialists' use the concept of the absurd as, partially at least, a technical term with a very specific meaning. These days, when we find something someone else says completely outrageous, we are likely to respond by saying, 'Don't be absurd!' And while there is nothing wrong with using the word this way – as a way of saying something like, 'That's so outrageous, it's not only false but completely beyond the pale!' – the Existentialists mean something else by it. For them, to say that something is absurd is to say that it contradicts reason. They thus use the word in a very precise way and I shall now explore how the Existentialists came to think it important to use the word 'absurd' in just this manner.

The meaning of life

The most well-known Existentialist claim involving the notion of the absurd is that life is absurd. What exactly does this mean? To understand this assertion, it will be helpful to contrast it with its opposite, namely the contention that life possesses a meaning. For many people, the puzzle about life's meaning – whether it has one and, if so, what that meaning is – is one of the chief impetuses to the study of philosophy.

Within a traditional Judeo–Christian–Islamic perspective – though not Kierkegaard's revolutionary one – there is a clear answer to this question: life's purpose is to fulfill God's commandments, often in hope of being rewarded in the after-life. The metaphysical assumptions behind such a view are not hard to discover. God, it is thought, made human beings with a certain purpose in mind. In this respect, human beings are taken to be similar to many of the objects that we ourselves create. Think about a knife. Its purpose is to cut. To be a knife is to be something that fulfills this function. As a result, we say that a knife's essence – by which we mean that which makes a knife a knife and not, say, a spoon, its ability to cut – precedes its existence. When someone makes an actual knife, they are attempting to create something that will fulfill the purpose that knives have, to make something whose existence realizes the essence of 'knifeness.'

Many traditional religious views – though not all – share a *teleological* conception of humans. The word 'teleological' comes from the Greek word *telos*, meaning 'end.' A teleological view of something treats it as created in order to fulfill a specific goal or end. So, to stick to the example of a knife, our conception of knives is teleological, for they are designed and produced in order to fulfill the goal of cutting. Now, it may seem odd to assert that, from a religious point of view, there is very little difference between the being of people and knives, but that's exactly what emerges when we look at the underlying conception of the being of both entities from a traditional religious perspective. In both cases, the entities are created for a purpose. Of course, the purpose of humans is a lot more complex and varied than the purpose of knives. One conception of God's purpose in creating humans, as I mentioned earlier, is for them to follow his rules for the conduct of life such as the Ten Commandments. If we accept this view of the purpose of human existence, then we know what we have to do with our lives, where their meaning will come from: observing all the rules that God has set forth in the Bible. The quest to fulfill those Commandments is what gives meaning to the lives of those who accept such a religious outlook. Since they know that that is what they are to do, they are able to see their lives as being *for* something, as having a meaning.

It should be obvious that the Existentialists reject this conception of life's meaning. At a basic level, they think that this view radically misconceives the nature of humans. As my examples have made clear, a teleological view of human beings assimilates them to artifacts, things that are made with a specific end in view, such as a knife. Of course, not all artifacts are as simple as knives. A house, for example, is a highly complex artifact, one that satisfies a range of needs, not just that of providing shelter. Still, even complex artifacts exist to fulfill the purposes for which they were created. And it is not just the being of humans that is assimilated to that of artifacts on the religious view, for God is also conceived on analogy with human artisans who make things to fulfill human needs, as Sartre noted in his essay 'Existentialism is a Humanism.' God becomes the Grand Artificer, for he makes humans for a purpose.

I have already mentioned what is probably the second most famous Existentialist slogan: 'Man's existence precedes his essence,' which also comes from Sartre's essay. The point of his claim is precisely to undermine a teleological view of human beings. By saying that we exist before we have an essence, Sartre reverses the relationship that holds between those concepts in the case of artifacts. His slogan thus reflects the basic Existentialist contention that humans, unlike all other entities in the world, are free to create themselves in accordance with their own desires. Our freedom means that we do not have any essence, any nature, that is given to us from outside ourselves, as we would have were the teleological conception of humans true.

Of course, the traditional theist has a reply at hand. He would contend against the Existentialists that our being free does not show that the teleological conception is wrong. Indeed, many theists think that God gave us our freedom in order to see if we would fulfill his commandments. We don't have to do this, but we have the ability to and, indeed, our purpose is just that, although we can fail and, when we do, we create ourselves as undeserving of God's mercy. So against the Existentialists' critique, the theist would insist that he has not underestimated the importance of freedom in human life.

Now the Existentialists would respond that such a view of life is odd in the extreme. What sense would it make, they would ask, for someone to create something with a free will only in order to see if it would act the way you wanted it to? Why not just create things with instincts, such as the lower animals like my dog, whose behavior is completely determined? Such a view of how life gets its meaning does not seem very coherent to the Existentialists. In fact, it leaves things at least as puzzling as they were before we started philosophizing about life's meaning in the first place.

Philosophers have sought to identify the 'goods,' that is, things we desire, whose possession could constitute the purpose of life. One obvious example is pleasure. Since everyone desires to have things that please them, why not admit that attaining significant and lasting pleasure is the goal of life? And there is a lot that recommends this view. After all, many of us regard working as a necessary evil, something we do only because of the rewards we receive for doing it. What we get from working, on this view, is generally money, which we use to buy not just the things we need, but the things we enjoy. So even work, on this view, is something we engage in for the pleasure it ultimately makes possible. People differ on what brings them pleasure. Some may like going to the movies, others lying on the beach. But, so the argument runs, whenever you pursue a specific activity, you are doing so because of the pleasure it brings you. And, if this is so, isn't pleasure the end that we all pursue, so that it is the thing that gives our lives their meaning?

Interesting as this idea is, many people find it unsatisfying. There must be, they feel, more to life than simply the pursuit of pleasurable activities. Think about the complex structure of our society, the years of schooling that we undergo, all the different jobs there are. Does all this exist simply to assist people in attaining pleasure? And even if it did, is pleasure all there is to life? There are pills that make people happy, but we don't think that living a meaningful life is simply a matter of taking a suitable number of the right pleasure-inducing pills. We seem to want something more, some deeper meaning from our existence. This is especially true if we think, as many contemporary people do, that there is no afterlife, that all that we have are the lives we live on this Earth. Acknowledging the fact of our own finitude leads not just to anxiety, but also to a quest for meaning, something to give us reassurance in the face of our own mortality.

Living the absurd

It is in this context that the Existentialist claim that life is absurd acquires its significance. In response to the attempt to find some hidden meaning that could provide the definitive answer to the deep and troubling question of our existence, the Existentialists deny that there is such an answer. The clearest exponent of this view is Albert Camus (see text box). He makes this claim in an attempt to undercut all the attempts to find a specific meaning for our existence. By claiming that life is absurd, Camus intends to deny the possibility that there is a meaning just waiting to be discovered. But despite what appears to be a depressing view of human life, Camus takes it to be affirmative. So we need to look more closely at exactly how this can be.

Albert Camus (1913–1960) was an Algerian-born novelist, playwright, and philosopher. Although Camus rejected the label 'Existentialist,' his ideas are closely linked to theirs and he was part of Sartre's 'circle' until they broke over Camus's rejection of the Communist Party (of which he, unlike Sartre, had formerly been a member). Camus was awarded the Nobel Prize for Literature in 1957.

Like many of the Existentialists, Camus wrote in a variety of different genres. Among his novels are *The Stranger* (1941) and *The Plague* (1947). The former is the story of a Frenchman living in northern Africa who kills an Arab for no ostensible reason. During his imprisonment, the man reflects on his guilt and responsibility. *The Plague* is an allegorical novel about the rise of Nazism.

Camus also wrote plays, including *Caligula* (1938), and philosophical essays including *The Myth of Sisyphus* (1942) and *The Rebel* (1951). Camus saw the act of rebellion or revolt as a crucial means of self-realization in an absurd world.

Because of the accessibility of his writings, Camus played a major role in the spread of Existentialism to a broad public. The Cure's song 'Killing an Arab,' is based on *The Stranger*.

Camus presents his distinctive conception of the absurd in his book *The Myth of Sisyphus*. For Camus, neither the world nor the human being by itself is absurd. The absurd comes into existence only through the juxtaposition of the two. On Camus's account, the assertion that life is absurd makes sense only when viewed as a claim about the lack of fit between human beings and the world they inhabit.

To understand Camus's view, we need to recall some themes we've already encountered. In the first chapter of this book, I discussed Sartre's contention that most things have the character of being precisely what they are, of existing *in-themselves*. With the notable exception of consciousness, everything is simply what it is. We also saw that the term that Sartre used to characterize this mode of existence was *facticity*, a term that is meant to indicate that there is no more to the being of certain things than their brute existence. A consequence of this, according to Camus, is that it does not make sense to claim that the world is in-itself either rational or irrational. It just proceeds along on its own way, without regard to anything else.

Of course, it's hard for humans to accept this view of the world. We have a tendency, for example, to personify the natural world. After a disastrous storm in which many people lose their lives, it seems obvious to many that nature is *cruel*. But when we attribute cruelty to something, we presuppose that that thing is a feeling agent with the capacity to be insensitive to the pain it causes. A child who tortures a puppy and gets pleasure from doing so can legitimately be called cruel, but an ice cream cone that falls apart before a child can eat it is not, since the ice cream cone lacks the capacity to feel or do anything. Nature, even though it has the capacity to cause a huge amount of pain and suffering, should not be thought of as cruel, since it is not cognizant of the effects it has on human beings. Nature is not a conscious agent and thus is not capable of cruelty or its opposite, compassion. It's even a mistake to say that nature is indifferent, for this suggests that nature has that very minimal attitude toward what happens, one situated midway between cruelty and compassion, as if it just didn't really care what its effects on human beings were. Nature is simply incapable of having any attitude about what it brings about. It simply is what it is.

In the first chapter, we also saw that human beings are for-themselves, that is, are conscious of their own mode of existence. Camus avoids the abstract metaphysical language that Sartre seems to revel in. For him, the most important ontological fact about human beings is that they inherently demand that things make sense, that the world be rational. What Camus means is that we want the things that happen in the world to be comprehensible by us, even if we don't like the results. One phenomenon that supports this view is the ubiquitous and seemingly incessant question that our young children ask when confronted with any new fact or phenomenon: 'Why?' Why is the sky blue? Why do I have to listen to you? Why does 2+2=4? Why is stealing wrong? These are just a few examples of the myriad questions young children ask. What we need to realize, on Camus's view, is that this persistent questioning reflects a demand that is characteristic of human beings, namely that the world make sense to us in terms we can understand.

If we put Camus's conception of the natural world as mere facticity together with his view of the need for comprehension we have as human beings, the inherent lack of fit between the two emerges. The world is just not the sort of thing that can fulfill our demand that it make sense to us, accord with the dictates of our reason. The project of science is, of course, to understand the world, but it does not do so in a way that Camus thinks can fulfill our desire for meaning. As I have said, many things happen in the world that don't make sense to us from our human point of view, even if they are capable – and many of them may not be – of being explained scientifically. The just are punished and the unjust are rewarded; the innocent suffer and the guilty prosper; and so on. Does this mean that the world is absurd? No, responds Camus, what's absurd is that we are creatures who demand reasonableness of a universe that does not, that cannot provide it. What's absurd is the lack of fit between a world that does not suit our expectation of receiving satisfying answers to our questions and our demand that it meet that very expectation. Life is absurd because we find ourselves in a world that is not suited to our need for it to make sense to us.

To see what is truly innovative about Camus's claims, we need to understand the importance that the concept of reason or rationality had in the Western philosophical tradition. Some have asserted that the notion of reason having a special place in the life of human beings is nearly coextensive with philosophy itself. As far back as the Ancient Greeks, the human being was defined as a *rational* animal, so that this specific feature of human beings was treated as the essential one, that which distinguished us from other animals. We have already seen that the Existentialists reject any categorization of humans that treats us as continuous with other types of existing things, so they hold that emphasizing the fact that we are animals, of whatever sort, was just a way to obscure our unique nature as *existing* beings. But it is no less true that they find the privileging of rationality in this standard definition deeply problematic. Human beings have many characteristics: we are feeling, caring, active creatures. To treat rationality as if it were the one feature that captures what is distinctive about us as creatures was, in their view, a huge mistake.

But perhaps even more significant is their objection to the attempt to treat rationality as something that was visible in the world itself. Philosophically, the question of the role of reason in human life had become a fundamental issue during the Enlightenment (see text box overleaf). The Enlightenment thinkers were flush with the success of the natural sciences at understanding the nature of the world. As a result, they reaffirmed reason – the capacity that they took to lie at the center of scientific investigation – as deserving pride of place in our understanding of the world.

The German philosopher G.W.F. Hegel represents the highpoint of this celebration of reason within the Western philosophical tradition despite his unorthodox interpretation of

The Enlightenment was an important European intellectual movement that began in the seventeenth century. Its hallmark was the fight against all forms of superstition and idolatry. It waged this war with the weapon of reason, which it took to provide the key for understanding the universe and ordering human affairs.

Most Enlightenment figures believed that Western civilization had made a significant break with all other cultures because of the discovery of scientific rationality. The natural sciences, they believed, provided us with the ability to gain unprecedented knowledge about how the natural world worked, knowledge that could be harnessed to the fulfillment of human needs. It is the application of scientific rationality to the problems of human social life that is the central legacy of the Enlightenment. Progress could now be achieved in the structuring of the human world because a new key for developing those structures had been discovered scientifically.

There was no single attitude that the Enlightenment figures took to traditional religion. Although many criticized it as a form of irrationalism, others attempted to find a rational basis for religious belief, one that fit with the modern scientific outlook the Enlightenment promoted. In its time, the Enlightenment was a progressive movement that sought to create a less arbitrary and unjust social order.

Among the leading figures in the Enlightenment we find: in France, René Descartes and Voltaire; in the United Kingdom, John Locke and David Hume; in Germany, Gottfried Leibniz and Immanuel Kant. The framers of the American Declaration of Independence – most prominently Benjamin Franklin and Thomas Jefferson – were deeply influence by the Enlightenment.

reason itself. 'The real is rational, the rational is real,' stands as the motto of Hegel's thought and asserts that existence is completely comprehensible through the categories of rational thought. Arguing in the tradition of Leibniz, but developing that great thinker's abstract understanding of the role of reason in the world, Hegel thought it was possible to discern the presence of a rational core in all of the world's developments. But, unlike Leibniz, Hegel was very clear that his vision was not one of facile optimism. Built into his dialectical conception of reality is an acknowledgment that every development contains within itself a 'negative moment,' that is, the seeds to its own destruction. However, Hegel's optimism is reflected in his belief that every negation contains within itself the seeds of the next positive development. As a result, he is able to affirm not only that everything that takes place does so for a reason, but that ultimately even the worst aspects of human history will be seen to have played a role in the progressive course of world affairs.

Kierkegaard found such a worldview preposterous and, so, articulated his own philosophical point of view through a thoroughgoing critique of its shortcomings. Most centrally, Kierkegaard rejected Hegel's conception of an increasingly rational world picture. In particular, the devout Dane opposed Hegel's treatment of religion as a cultural phenomenon that would ultimately be replaced by philosophy. His own conception of religious faith as inherently absurd can be seen as an attempt to save the phenomenon of religion from its incorporation into Hegel's omnivorous dialectic. It was an endeavor to keep the individual and particular features of a human life from being swallowed up into the universal and general. Although Hegel himself maintained that he had found a way of doing justice to the individual in the context of the universal, Kierkegaard thought that attempt a complete failure.

In developing this line of thought, Kierkegaard set up a framework to which all subsequent Existentialists gave their allegiance. But what they accepted was not the viability of the religious worldview Kierkegaard held so dear; instead, they found inspiration in his rejection of Hegel's view that human life and conduct have a rational basis. The tradition that Kierkegaard founded is united in its denial that our lives have such a rational foundation and its affirmation of the significance of the absurd. Camus's particular innovation was to apply the concept of absurdity to life itself, to show that the desire for rationality was simply incapable of satisfaction by the world in which we live.

At this point, one of the criticisms often made of Existentialism recurs: that it emphasizes the negative side of human life. In the previous chapters, we surveyed some of the things that give this criticism its bite, such as the Existentialists' general emphasis on anxiety as the most metaphysically signifi-cant human emotion and Ivan's specific focus on the cruel acts perpetrated by human beings against children. Now we find Camus claiming that life is absurd, that our desire to find meaning is doomed to failure. If we add in Sartre's well-known statement that man is a useless passion, it seems that Existentialist thinkers of all stripes are guilty of negativity.

And yet, we need to note the affirmative side of Existentialism that this critical assessment fails to acknowledge. Nowhere is this clearer than in Camus's claim that we must imagine Sisyphus happy. Sisyphus, you will recall, is the mythi-cal Greek hero who was condemned by Zeus to eternally roll a huge rock up a mountain. Although there are various different accounts of why Zeus gave Sisyphus this particular punishment, they all emphasize Sisyphus's disobedience and his love of life. So, every time Sisyphus gets close to completing his task – as he approaches the summit – the rock evades his control and falls back down the mountain, forcing Sisyphus himself to descend and begin his eternal task once more. Although we may feel our lives to be difficult and unfulfilling because we are engaged in activities that have no ultimate meaning, our complaints pale when compared to Sisyphus's lot. He stands as a symbol of the idea of an absurd life, a life without meaning and satisfaction, a life whose central task can never be completed satisfactorily.

But Camus ends his discussion of Sisyphus with the following startling claim: 'One must imagine Sisyphus happy.' How can this be? Camus's answer is that Sisyphus is happy because he scorns the gods and 'there is no fate that cannot be surmounted by scorn.' To explain, Camus asks us to think about Sisyphus at the moment when the rock has fallen back to earth and he must descend to begin his task anew. What is he thinking, feeling? I take Camus to imagine Sisyphus thinking something like this: 'Oh no! There goes that darn rock again. I guess I've got to go down and retrieve it again. That dumb old Zeus! How could he even think of such a thing? Who does he think he is? Well, he can't defeat me. I'm just going to go back and start all over again just to spite him!'

If this inner dialogue makes sense, we can see why Camus thinks that Sisyphus is happy. His scorn for Zeus and the fate to which he has been consigned allows him to take control of his own situation. Although Zeus has the power to condemn him to an eternally unachievable task, he does not have control of Sisyphus's mind. So, instead of seeing himself as a victim of a cruel fate as Zeus would like, Sisyphus is able to choose a different way of interpreting his situation, one that is characterized by complete scorn for his 'master.' Although Sisyphus's scornful reaction is predicated on his realization that he will never succeed at his designated task, he is nonetheless able to free himself from a sense of defeat and succeed at what Camus calls 'living in the absurd.'

With this reimagining of the myth of Sisyphus, Camus gives his answer to the question of why suicide does not make sense as a response to the recognition of life's absurdity, the philosophical problem he characterized as the lone serious one. Although Camus asserts that suicide is self-defeating because it destroys the absurdity of life by canceling one of the two terms that are necessary for its existence, I think there is a deeper answer that his perspective provides. Were one to kill oneself, one would be defeated by one's situation. But there is a way to avoid such a fate, a way not to be defeated by the absurdity of the circumstances in which one finds oneself. One can accept that fate and, in being scornful of it, achieve the sort of happiness that is available to us as human beings.

Absurd thinkers

Camus's discussion of the absurdity of human life has given rise to a great deal of philosophical discussion – and not just among avowed Existentialists. The contemporary Analytic philosopher, Thomas Nagel, for example, agrees that life is absurd, but thinks that Camus's analysis of that absurdity is mistaken. For Nagel, what's absurd is that we vacillate between two different perspectives on our own activities. When we are involved in doing something, we normally think that we are doing something worthwhile. If I'm a violinist, I have to think that there's something significant about playing the violin or I won't be able to engage in the strenuous practice sessions required to become skilled. To engage in anything, Nagel says, we need to take that activity or pursuit *seriously*. But it is also true that human beings can step back from their own activities and concerns and take a more detached point of view. If I think about the fact that I am just one human being on a planet in one solar system in a vast galaxy that is but a small part of an unimaginably huge universe, my own violin playing just won't seem something that makes any difference at all. Indeed, from such a point of view – that often attributed to God? – maybe human life as a whole is just a small blip on the screen, so to speak. I remember going to the new Hayden Planetarium in New York with my son. When you leave, you descend a huge spiral ramp that represents the history of the universe. At the bottom, there is a mark only the width of a human hair that represents the entire history of the human race. If you think about your life from such an astronomical perspective, it's hard to take very much of what happens seriously. What's absurd, according to Nagel, is that we can always take such a detached perspective on any of our activities, one from which nothing appears to have any real significance. No matter what we choose to do, we can always see it as something that is not worth taking seriously.

Nagel also criticizes Camus's solution to the problem of suicide. He thinks that scorn is not the appropriate attitude to take to the absurdity of life when that absurdity is understood as a conflict between two necessary perspectives. All we can do is realize that any project in which we choose to invest ourselves can be seen from a detached perspective as no better than anything else. But this realization accords with the position of an *ironist*, someone who always sees her own commitments as arbitrary and contingent.

Another dimension to the Existentialist analysis of life's absurdity can be found in the writings of Franz Kafka (1883–1924), who, in his great novels and stories, investigates the absurdity of our faith in reason in light of the bureaucratization of modern life. Kafka's novel *The Trial* (1925) tells the story of a man, identified only as K., who keeps looking for a rational explanation for his being summoned to a trial when he has done nothing wrong. K. has led a life in which he has done nothing to bring him under suspicion and yet suspect he is. In Kafka's brilliant portrayal, we see a man attempting to understand the nature of a reality that will not permit any rational explanations for what is taking place. What we see in *The Trial* is how deep-seated our need for a rational explanation of our lives is.

Kafka's writings have often been interpreted as a response to the increased bureaucratization of life in Western societies.

What he realized, and gave life to in his fictions, is the unique 'logic' belonging to bureaucracies. When human beings, with their own needs, desires, and standards, come into contact with a bureaucracy, they find themselves having to conform to a world whose practices are incompatible with their own need for reasonableness. These days, even a simple phone call to a corporation places us into an endless labyrinth of button pushing and waiting, as a vaguely human-sounding computer voice gives us our options: 'If you having a billing problem, push 1; if you have a technical problem, push 2,' and so on. Wanting to talk to a human being, we find ourselves in a maze of computerized options, with our hope of finding a sympathetic understanding seemingly endlessly deferred. The nightmare of a totally bureaucratized world has acquired dimensions of which Kafka could not even dream in his nightmarish vision.

But for the Existentialists, these social developments – from the bureaucratization of the law to the computerization of the phone service – only make the absurdity of life more apparent. From their point of view, the world never suited our needs or desires, a claim for which they find ample support in history. We have already seen how Camus finds precedent for his view of the absurdity of life in the Greek myth of Sisyphus, but he also references Oedipus as an absurd hero who lived out his fate even as he sought to avoid it. In addition, we noted how Kierkegaard turns to the Old Testament to find confirmation for his conception of the religious life as founded on absurdity. And even Sartre, who used the Greek myth of Orestes' murder of his mother as the basis for his play *The Flies*, finds in Greek mythology another anticipation of this fundamental Existentialist theme.

Thus life's absurdity, though made more evident for the Existentialists by the developments of the past two centuries, is a fact about the nature of human life on the planet. While they would admit that people have been made more aware of the absurdity of their lives by changes in the circumstances they confront, the Existentialists reject the attempt to localize it to a specific time and place. For the Existentialists, such attempts are only a last ditch effort to avoid accepting what cannot in good conscience be denied: that our aspirations for our own lives cannot find satisfaction in the world as we find it.

The absurdity of life is also a theme that recurs in many literary and theatrical works. Samuel Beckett's *Waiting for Godot* (1954) initiated a theatrical movement that was termed 'theater of the absurd' and had historical links to Existentialism. Imagine the surprise of theater goers accustomed to seeing works like *Hamlet* or Ibsen's *A Doll's House* who find themselves confronted with two tramps, Vladimir and Estragon, on a stage empty but for one dead tree, waiting for the arrival of a figure, Godot, who never appears. As the two tramps wait upon their dump, they interact with each other in ways that remind us of our own lives, only the absurdity of their situation is even more pronounced, for it lacks the 'concrete filling' that we use to embroider our lives; all that we see on stage is two characters who are attempting to fill up their time with various distractions as they wait for death.

This apparently bleak vision of human life struck many viewers as rooted in Existentialism. The tramps' eternal wait is similar to ours, as we wonder whether there is a God and what we are doing here on earth. Their repeatedly failed attempts to find a meaningful activity or even conversational topic seem to shed a searing light upon all of our attempts to find projects that we think will give our lives meaning and significance.

Ingmar Bergman's masterful film *Persona* (1966) also has deep affinities with the Existential recognition of the absurdity of life. In the film, a great actress, Elisabeth Vogler (Liv Ullman), stops speaking in the midst of a performance of Sophocles' tragedy *Electra*, and refuses to talk again. Alma (Bibi Anderson), the nurse who is sent to care for Elisabeth, tries to understand what led her to make this difficult decision. Among the hypotheses that Alma arrives at is Elisabeth's recognition that nothing makes sense, that, in the words of the Existentialists, life is absurd. Although there is a great deal more to the film – it depicts the dissolution of Alma's personality as she comes more and more to resemble Elisabeth – it is permeated with a sense of life's absurdity and the difficulty of finding a way of existing that one can adopt without hypocrisy.

A more recent film that explores these notions is Sam Mendes' 1999 film *American Beauty*, in which Lester Burnham (Kevin Spacey) is a suburbanite caught in the midst of a mid-life crisis. He realizes that he is just going through the paces in every aspect of his life: his job is unfulfilling; his marriage a joke; his daughter hates him; no aspect of his life seems untainted by absurdity, its failure to accord with his hopes and aspirations for it. The aestheticism the film finally opts for bears no resemblance to Camus's starker vision, yet it remains a plausible attempt to confront the dilemma of life's absurdity.

These traces of the Existentialists' conception of the absurdity of life in both 'high' and 'low' art show how influential this theme has been within Western culture generally. These works have helped us see how hollow traditional rationalizations of human existence have proved to be in the modern world. The Existentialist notion that we live in a world that denies us the satisfactions that we seek has been very attractive, despite the negative connotations that it has. In part, this is because, rather than be defeated by this most difficult of truths, the Existentialists ask us to affirm our humanity triumphantly, 'for crushing truths perish from being acknowledged,' as Camus puts it (*Myth of Sisyphus*, 122). The absurdity of life is not, on their view, a reason to despair, but the grounds for living life authentically, a theme to which I turn in the next chapter.

7

Authenticity

The lead character of Marc Forster's 2006 film *Stranger than Fiction*, Harold Crick (Will Ferrell) is an odd duck. An IRS auditor, he lives a life that seems guided in almost cookbook fashion by rules for dealing with every situation he encounters. As a way of representing what his life is like, the film makes the content of his obsessive way of thinking visible on the screen, overlaying a normal photographic shot of him performing different actions with opaque white writing that represents his mental functioning. We see him in the picture on this page, for example, tying his tie by following, in almost computer-like fashion, a set of explicit instructions for how to do so.

Figure 3 *Stranger Than Fiction* (2006) Marc Forster, director; Sony Pictures

From an Existentialist point of view, Crick is paradigmatic of the alienated individual, for he is out of touch with all the important features of his own experience as a human being, living a life according to a set of instructions that he has internalized and missing out on the sorts of experiences that most people think make life worth living.

But things in this film are not exactly what they seem. Although it appears to be employing the standard cinematic technique of a voice-over narrator, who is not part of the world of the fiction, to describe what is taking place, we soon discover that Crick himself can hear the narration, a fact that indicates that it must emanate from the film's fictional world. (Film scholars call this a 'diegetic' use of sound.) This is puzzling because we had been assuming that the voice-over narrator is talking to us, the film's audience, so that the characters in the fictional world of the film could not hear what she is saying. (And, if this were true, the sound would have been 'non-diegetic.') In that case, her words would have described the fictional world from outside, so to speak, rather than being spoken from within it. As a result of this apparent transgression of the boundary between fiction and reality, we are confused about exactly what is taking place.

Eventually, it becomes clear, both to Crick and to us, that the voice we are hearing is that of Karen Eiffel (Emma Thompson), a well-known author of novels whose literary trademark is killing the heroes of her books. This is, of course, not good news to Crick, for it means that he is certain to die unless he can somehow manage to change the pattern of Eiffel's fiction. The result of this interesting cinematic move is that the voice-over narration is actually spoken by a character within the world of the film, so that fiction and reality merge as we realize that Crick and Eiffel inhabit the same world.

I begin this chapter with a discussion of *Stranger than Fiction* because it is the best example I know of a film that illustrates how anticipating one's own demise can lead to a profound transformation of one's life. This is an important theme of Existentialism that was developed most importantly by Martin Heidegger in *Being and Time*, albeit with a set of quite difficult theoretical concepts. The crucial claim of his account is that anticipating one's own death can transform one from living an alienated life structured in conformity to the standards of others to achieving an authentic life in which one's own values are paramount. Since we have already seen in some detail how the Existentialists characterize the human tendency toward social conformity, it's high time to explore the notion of authenticity.

Essentially, an authentic life is one lived in full acknowledgment of one's freedom as a human being to choose how to conduct one's life. Although it may be difficult to judge in actual practice whether one is pursuing a course of action because one is freely choosing it or because it is the socially acceptable thing to do, the theoretical distinction between these two types of motivations is clear. Sometimes, as we have seen, people do things because other people approve of their doing them. When I, to return to an earlier example, put on a tie and jacket to teach, I did so because my colleagues wanted me to. But there are times when one does something because it is what one truly wants and one knows that one has the freedom to make such choices for oneself. This type of rationale stands out clearly when a person is ostracized for doing something that transgresses social norms. For example, we can imagine the case of a young woman who identifies as a feminist, but decides to give up her plans for graduate school to live with the man she loves and raise a family because that is what she really wants to do. In this case, the young woman would have chosen to do what she actually wished to, despite the fact that she might have been ostracized by her feminist friends who thought that choice the wrong one for her to make. This provides an example of an authentic act, even though one could go on to investigate the source of the woman's desire to have a family to see if it was really as 'inner-directed' as it appears to be. Still, it helps us see the point of the Existentialists' distinction between conformist and authentic action, even as it highlights the difficulties of judging with certainty the character of any individual act.

In the history of philosophy, Socrates (469–399 BCE) stands out as an example of someone whose actions were authentically chosen. As he explains in the *Apology*, his defense at his trial for impiety, he has an inner voice – he calls it his *daemon* – which he hears when he is about to do something that his *daemon* knows to be wrong. When this happens, he listens to his inner voice and then acts as it counsels. This phenomenon is familiar to most of us as a 'pang of conscience,' something that we feel when we are acting in ways that we know to be wrong but want to do anyway, perhaps to get approval from our peers. It is this division between our normal ways of acting and those instigated by our inner voice that the Existentialists think has great significance.

But we have seen that the Existentialists believe that the self we initially encounter and remain in touch with for the most part is a conformist self, one that is formed through accepting the norms of others. If living a fulfilling life requires, as they think it does, coming to experience our true or authentic self – the nihilating self that is the source of our freedom as human beings – the question arises as to how we can become aware of it when our conformist self so dominates us that we are not even aware that there is more to us than that.

There are a variety of routes that allow a person to discover the possibility of authenticity, according to the Existentialists, and each results in the emergence of a self other than the alienated self of social conformism. One prominent path involves the experience of conscience that I just discussed. The difficulty we face in listening to this 'inner voice' is that it is so easy to ignore it, to see it as just providing yet another norm that we need not accept. A more definitive path is that provided by death, for the Existentialists – Martin Heidegger in particular – think that facing one's own death provides the force needed to extricate oneself from the 'dictatorship of the They,' as Heidegger so graphically terms it (*Being and Time*, 126).

Stranger than Fiction provides a clear illustration of this claim. Faced with his own death at the hands of Eiffel's pen, two things happen to Crick. First of all, he tries to do everything he can to avoid it. When he attempts to track down Eiffel in order to convince her to spare him, the film plays up a variety of comic exchanges, since all of the interactions between these two characters involve a transgression of the barrier between fiction and reality within the film's fictional world. This gives rise to misunderstandings that are a source of a great deal of the film's humor. But, more significantly from our point of view, Crick also starts to change how he lives. Faced with the imminence of his own death and the anxiety the anticipation of it causes him, his highly efficient life begins to seem cramped and limiting to him. Fearing that he will soon meet his own demise, he realizes that all the things he has not done will remain forever beyond his reach. This realization allows him to break out of his stifling routine as an IRS auditor and reject his own subjection to the demands of his conformist self. In place of its constraints, he begins to lead a life that is attuned to needs and desires of which he was previously unaware. In so doing, he expands his sense of the life-options available to him. In particular, he woos a counter-cultural baker, Ana Pascal (Maggie Gyllenhall), and generally sheds his former, completely inhibited self in pursuit of a more expansive and authentic life. He even comes to accept his fate, although Eiffel herself has second thoughts about condemning him to death, and eventually gives him a reprieve.

Although *Stranger than Fiction* is basically a light-hearted romp played for comic effect, it nicely illustrates how the anticipation of one's own death can lead one to reject social conformity in favor of Existentialist authenticity. When we first meet Crick, he is a parody of the conformist person, so deeply has the need to do what is expected of him permeated every aspect of his being. (Ironically, such hyper-conformity turns into a type of non-conformity.) But through the anxiety caused by his discovery of the imminence of his own demise – a discovery he makes as a result of also finding out that he is a character in a fiction – he jettisons his allegiance to constrictive social norms and starts to build a more authentic life for himself. The twin discomfiting experiences of hearing a voice in his head and having to confront his own death get Crick to realize that he has the potential to live a more complete, a more fulfilling, indeed a more authentic life.

Facing death squarely

Stranger Than Fiction thus provides a good introduction to the Existentialist thesis that a person's anticipation of his own death can provide the fulcrum by means of which to achieve a more authentic existence. But there are many aspects of the Existentialists' claims about authenticity that the film deals with only glancingly, if at all. As I explore Heidegger's own existential analysis of being-towards-death, I want to illustrate his claims through a careful examination of some additional aspects of 'The Death of Ivan Ilych,' for Tolstoy's story provides an excellent illustration of a number of the themes Heidegger sounds concerning death and authenticity.

'The Death of Ivan Ilych' presents a careful and nuanced version of the Existentialists' dichotomy between a conformist and an authentic self as well as the role that the anticipation of one's own death can play in the achievement of authenticity. Tolstoy's way of characterizing Ilych's life sums his conformity up with terrifying acuity: 'Ivan Ilych's life had been most simple and most ordinary and therefore most terrible.' What makes this life so awful is precisely Ilych's near exclusive focus on the opinion of others, so that he structures his life in accordance with the norms that he takes them to endorse. Tolstoy describes him as 'a capable, cheerful, good-natured, and sociable man, though strict in the fulfillment of what he considered to be his duty: and he considered his duty to be what was so considered by those in authority' ('The Death of Ivan Ilych,' 105). This is an accurate description of what Heidegger describes as a 'dictatorship of the They,' for Ilych seeks to live according to the opinions of those who have power over him. All of his opinions are formed to match their standards. But Ilych does not think of himself as someone who lives by others' norms, for he has *internalized* them. What he experiences as his duty is simply the internalized social norms of his superiors. Tolstoy thus enriches our sense of how others' standards come to have such a strong hold on us, for they appear to us as if they were nothing but our own values.

Although Ilych's conformist self appears to be in complete possession of his being, he still hears the whispers of his authentic self. But rather than listen to this voice in a Socratic fashion, Ilych learns how to silence it:

> At school he had done things which had formerly seemed to him very horrid and made him feel disgusted with himself when he did them; but when later on he saw that such actions were done by people of good position and they did not regard them as wrong, he was able not exactly to regard them as right, but to forget about them entirely and not be at all troubled at remembering them. ('The Death of Ivan Ilych,' 105)

Tolstoy here describes what Heidegger terms the *tranquillization* of one's conscience by the They. Ilych certainly had a conscience as a student, for he felt bad about behaving badly. But when he noticed that the people he admired did things that he did not approve of, he changed his own standards of conduct so that they come more closely into line with the behavior of others. Or, more precisely, he didn't change his standards, so much as he simply silenced his own conscience by what Tolstoy characterizes as an act of willful forgetting. In so doing, he satisfied the demands that others made on him for his conformity, while also losing touch with the quiet promptings of his authentic self.

As time goes on, every aspect of Ilych's life comes to be lived as his conformist self demands. He wears the 'right' clothes that he buys at the right stores; he eats at the right restaurants; and, in general, he behaves as one who aspires to be a member of the social group of powerful people he admires. His friends are not those whose company he enjoys, but those who come from the 'best' circle of the legal profession and wealthy aristocrats. He marries Praskovya Fëdorovna Mikhel not so much because he loves her, but because 'it was considered the right thing by the most highly placed of his associates' ('The Death of Ivan Ilych,' 109). In all things, Ivan Ilych is concerned to live a life of 'pleasant lightheartedness and decorum,' one that suits the norms he perceives to be those of the best circles of society.

Tolstoy's description of Ivan Ilych provides us with a searingly critical portrait of the conformist. Although a conformist accommodates himself to the demands he takes others to make on him, Tolstoy shows how such a person might fail to experience himself as yielding to the opinions of others because Their norms can become internalized as his own. Indeed, such internalization can become so powerful that the authentic self is completely silenced, its presence forgotten in the dim recesses of one's memory.

This raises a concern about the Existentialists' notion of an authentic self. As Tolstoy describes it – and Heidegger endorses and follows him in this respect – the authentic self is there, in the deepest recesses of our being, awaiting our discovery and acknowledgment. But other Existentialists – Nietzsche and Sartre are the prime examples of this – see the authentic self as something one has to create for oneself through a rejection of the social norms that constitute the inauthentic self. For these philosophers, talk of an authentic self does not commit one to its pre-existence, for this self is an achievement rather than a discovery. Fortunately, we do not have to decide which of these two accounts of the authentic self is more accurate. It is sufficient for us to note that the Existentialists themselves were divided about the ontological status of the authentic self despite their agreement about its significance.

Regardless of what one decides about the status of the authentic self, there is another question for which 'The Death of Ivan Ilych' provides a compelling account: How can a person discover the inauthenticity of the conformist life he has led? In the case of Ilych, as in that of Crick, this happens through a confrontation with the fact of his own imminent death, one that discloses to him the possibility of living authentically. When Ilych learns that an injury to his kidney and appendix suffered while fixing up a newly acquired house is serious and will soon cause him to die, he has an insight that changes him profoundly, as he painfully comes to acknowledge the vacuity of the life he has led.

The first step in this process of self-revelation is that the anxiety caused by his awareness of his impending death separates Ilych from the others who meant so much to him.

> There was no deceiving himself: something terrible, new, and more important than anything before in his life, was taking place within him of which he alone was aware. Those about him did not understand or would not understand, but thought everything in the world was going on as usual. That tormented Ivan Ilych more than anything. ('The Death of Ivan Ilych,' 125)

What Ilych here discovers is something that we have already seen portrayed in *Stranger Than Fiction*: that one impetus to conformity is the denial of death. The very first scenes of Tolstoy's story show how Ilych's friends and even his wife fend off their acknowledgment of their own mortality – something that might have been occasioned by his death – by focusing on the importance of their everyday concerns, whether that is amusing oneself with cards or acting in a socially sanctioned manner. But once he had become aware that his death was imminent – what Heidegger calls the 'certain and as such indefinite, not to be outstripped [i.e., avoided]' character of our own death (*Being and Time*, 303) – those strategies of denial lost their attractiveness as his own impending death dominated his consciousness. He soon discovers that there is no one with whom he can share his concern: 'He had to live thus all alone on the brink of an abyss, with no one who understood or pitied him' ('The Death of Ivan Ilych,' 127). (Later, he finds a peasant youth to whom he can relate, but we can safely ignore this aspect of Tolstoy's romanticized vision of the Russian peasantry.)

Here, too, Tolstoy's account illustrates Heidegger's claims about death. For Heidegger, death – or, more fully, an authentic being-towards-death – individualizes *Dasein*, frees a person from their immersion in the They. The reason for this is that one's death is one's 'ownmost possibility.' Tolstoy's account of Ilych's isolation from others provides us with a clear way of envisioning the process that Heidegger characterizes so abstractly. Because his death has a unique significance for him – after all, only he will cease to be, even if others will miss him – the realization of this momentous fact separates Ilych from the others to whom he had previously been close. Nothing has happened to them, so they remain tied to their own conformist strategies of avoidance. But because Ilych has been transformed by his own acknowledgment of his mortality, he finds himself alone, separate from the others. He is becoming an *individual*.

The importance of being an individual is something that we have already noticed as central to Existentialist thought. Beginning with Kierkegaard's objection to what he took to be Hegel's valorization of the universal over and above the particular, the Existentialist tradition asserted the importance of achieving individuality. What Tolstoy's story adds to our understanding of the Existentialists' theory of individuality is that being an individual requires one to separate oneself from the conformity that dominates alienated sociality.

As the process of what we might call his 'authentification' progresses, Ilych becomes aware of the absurdity of life, albeit through what he takes to be the absurdity of his death. He realizes that the accident that will eventually kill him happened as he was trying to hang a curtain in his new home, something he now sees as completely trivial: 'It really is so! I lost my life over that curtain as I might have done when storming a fort. Is that possible? How terrible and how stupid. It can't be true! It can't, but it is' ('The Death of Ivan Ilych,' 134).

The contrast between the triviality of the cause of his illness – hanging a curtain – and the significance of what that illness entails for him – the end of his life – registers on Ilych as a symbol of life's absurdity. What strikes home to him is the wide gap between an actual event – his being hit in the side – and the significance it has for him – its bringing about his death. But this is precisely the sort of disjunction that Camus and others take as a sign of life's absurdity: we live in a world that does not accord with our own human expectations of it. That an ordinary, everyday occurrence can have deep and abiding consequences for the life of a human being is one mark of the absurd.

But Ilych's evolution doesn't simply stop with his recognition of life's absurdity; it continues as he re-evaluates his whole life. At first he is puzzled: 'It can't be that life is so senseless and horrible ... Maybe I did not live as I ought to have done ... But how could that be, when I did everything properly?' ('The

Death of Ivan Ilych,' 148). Still trapped in a conformist notion of what matters in life, Ilych here begins to see that the fact that one must die has crucial implications for how one should live one's life. What confuses him is that he has done everything 'properly.' What he means, of course, is that he has lived his life in accordance with the standards of the 'best' social group. To put his thought in other words, he wonders why, when he has done everything that is expected of him, he is left with the feeling that his life has been completely meaningless. What he can't understand is how his always having done 'the right thing' could have resulted in his feeling he had not lived correctly!

In order to resolve this puzzle, Ilych needs to countenance the idea that perhaps his whole life was premised on a mistake. And, indeed, this is precisely what he eventually realizes:

> It occurred to him that what had appeared perfectly impossible before, namely that he had not spent his life as he should have done, might after all be true. It occurred to him that his scarcely perceptible attempts to struggle against what was considered good by the most highly placed people, those scarcely notice-able impulses which he had immediately suppressed, might have been the real thing, and all the rest were false. And his professional duties and the whole arrangement of his life and of his family, and all his social and official interests, might all have been false. ('The Death of Ivan Ilych,' 152)

Tolstoy is here describing a process of self-transformation that lies at the heart of Existentialism. It is a process that Heidegger describes as *Dasein* freeing itself from the domination of the They and achieving an 'authentic potentiality-for-being.'

Let's reflect on how Tolstoy presents its dynamics. First, Ilych finally has the courage to entertain the notion that following the norms embraced by those in positions of social power is precisely what has made his life meaningless. Because he has lived his life completely for others in that he has, however unconsciously, sought their approval, he has denied his freedom as a human being. Second, the possibility of an alternative way of conducting his life was never completely extinguished in him, although he chose never to listen to its promptings. As we have seen and as he now recognizes, there were moments when he had viewed his own actions from a perspective different from that embraced by others, but he also realizes that he has squelched the very thing that could have provided his salvation: those promptings made by his own sense of what was right and proper. Ilych has, as it were, discovered what Heidegger terms 'the voice of conscience' that discloses the possibility of authentic existence.

So Tolstoy's story provides us with an excellent illustration of many of the key aspects of Heidegger's account of the role of death in achieving authenticity. Indeed, its compelling narrative makes that theory seem plausible and intuitively convincing. Still, there are aspects of the notion of authenticity that need to be addressed more fully than they are within the story and so we need to supplement it with a look at some of their more traditional philosophical texts. Consider, for example, the question of the proper way to characterize an action that is done authentically. We have said that an authentic action is one a person does in full awareness of her freedom, her existence as a nihilating being. A person who acts authentically thus has to accept complete responsibility for what she does, and not attribute the action to any form of influence or compulsion. In addition, one cannot engage in any form of Bad Faith, for these all involve self-attributions that in one way or another undermine one's freedom. But how can I tell if an action I perform is actually authentic?

Acting authentically

Friedrich Nietzsche, the great nineteenth-century German philosopher (see text box, p. 139), proposed an interesting test for determining whether an action was authentic. Instead of going the traditional route and asking whether something one does is moral, Nietzsche suggests the following: assume that everything that takes place in the history of the world will repeat itself an infinite number of times exactly as it has in the past or as it will in the future. If you want to go to the movies rather than do some work you need to do, or if you want to eat that chocolate pie despite being on a diet, imagine that you will have to relive the consequences of your decision in every one of the recurrences of the history of the world. This means that if you choose to work, you will miss that movie not just tonight, but in every 'tonight' that occurs an infinite number of times as the world repeats itself again and again. His idea was that the outcome of the test of 'the Eternal Recurrence of the Same,' as he calls this hypothesis, would be an action that was authentic. For, while it might be easy to give up a piece of pie right now, it would be difficult if not impossible to give it up an infinite number of times unless you were choosing that option authentically. (It is worth pointing out that Nietzsche's Eternal Recurrence test is an inversion of the Christian idea that you would be eternally damned for sinning. Nietzsche conceived of his own philosophy as a sort of anti-Christianity.)

Nietzsche's test brings us face to face with the question of the relationship between authenticity and traditional moral notions such as right and wrong. Within the Western tradition of philosophy, these are the primary concepts used to evaluate human actions. One of the central tasks of traditional ethics is thus to explain our justification for claiming certain actions are right, that they are ones we should perform.

The Existentialists believe that talk of actions being right or wrong should be replaced by the evaluation of actions in terms of their authenticity or lack of it. This is the upshot of their criticism of conformist behavior. The problem they see with such behavior is that it is legitimated by something external to an

Friedrich Nietzsche (1844–1900) was a prodigy who became a full professor at the University of Basel at the age of twenty-four. Unfortunately, poor health forced him to resign his position in 1879. For the rest of his life, he lived a nomadic existence, wandering from Switzerland to France and Italy. In 1889, he collapsed while watching a horse being cruelly whipped. He never fully recovered and died the following year.

Although Nietzsche's first book, *The Birth of Tragedy from the Spirit of Music* (1872), was written in a mostly academic style, his later writings are noted for their literary merit as well as philosophical insight. Using a wide range of styles, including aphorisms and myths as well as more straightforward philosophical prose, Nietzsche published a series of books in which he indicted Western society for its decadence and weakness. His analysis of pre-Socratic Greece showed the possibility of an alternative type of culture, one that was grounded on strength and self-affirmation. He held out hope for a renewal of Western society in which strong individuals would flourish. Among his books are *Thus Spake Zarathustra* (1883–1885), *Beyond Good and Evil* (1886), and *On the Genealogy of Morals* (1887).

After World War II, Nietzsche was often regarded as a precursor and defender of National Socialism (Nazism). In part, this is because his sister, Elisabeth Förster-Nietzsche, an avowed Nazi, edited an edition of his posthumous unpublished notes as *The Will to Power* (1901) and attempted to make it appear as if Nietzsche were himself anti-Semitic. In fact, he was not, and broke with the German composer Richard Wagner, over the latter's anti-Semitism.

individual human being, either the general consensus of a 'They' or the authority of a Grand Inquisitor. In either case, the individual has not had to reflect on and acknowledge the validity of the action itself, as the authentic person must do.

But this gives rise to a problem. If we are to evaluate the moral worth of an action in terms of its being or failing to be authentic, then it seems that we are only concerned with *how* a person chooses to perform an act and not with the content of the act itself. This is very different from more traditional moral evaluations, for these tend to focus on the content of acts. The Ten Commandments, to return to the obvious example of moral rules that I have invoked more than once, specify types of actions that are morally good, thus focusing on the nature of what is being done rather than its motivation. They tell us that we should perform certain types of actions, for example, honoring our father and mother, and avoid others, for example, murdering someone. What makes some actions morally worthy is their being 'parent-honoring' actions, independently of why one does them. But when we replace such traditional moral evaluations with ones based on authenticity, we move away from a focus on the type of action that is being performed to the motivation for performing it. (I should note that there are other moral theories, such as Kant's, that also focus on a person's motivation for performing an action in assessing its moral worth.) But this suggests that a person could have the right type of motivation for performing an action and still do something with a morally objectionable content.

To see why this portends a problem for the Existentialist theory of authenticity, consider the case of Adolf Hitler. Hitler's decision to exterminate all the Jews of Europe is a paradigm of a morally wrong action; indeed, one that is completely abhorrent. But in this thought experiment, let's assume that Hitler made that decision in full consciousness of his nature as a human being. So we will assume for the purposes of this discussion that Hitler sat down and thought about his nature as a free and nihilating being. He might even have read the relevant passages from Heidegger's *Being and Time*, since Heidegger was, at least for a time, a Nazi Party member and public servant. We will further assume that Hitler then decided that the Final Solution was something that he would initiate as a freely chosen project. It seems that the Existentialists would have to admit that such a morally reprehensible action would be, according to their own standards, an authentic one, and hence not subject to condemnation according to *their* criteria for assessing the moral worth of an action. If this is correct, it exposes a significant problem for the Existentialists, for it suggests that they lack an adequate means for evaluating the morality of actions. If something as heinous as the Final Solution could be characterized as authentic, then that criterion is not adequate as a means of assessing the moral worth of human actions.

I believe that Sartre recognized this problem and that is why he attempted to meld his Existentialist account of an action's morality with Kant's. What he says in 'Existentialism is a Humanism' is this:

> When we say that man chooses himself, we do mean that every one of us must choose himself; but by that we also mean that in choosing for himself he chooses for all men. For in effect, of all the actions a man may take in order to create himself as he wills to be, there is not one which is not creative, at the same time, of an image of man such as he believes he ought to be. To choose between this or that is at the same time to affirm the value of that which is chosen; for we are unable ever to choose the worse. What we choose is always the better; and nothing can be better for us unless it is better for all. ('Existentialism is a Humanism,' 291–2)

In this passage, Sartre begins with what we recognize as a statement of his Existentialist point of view: 'Man chooses himself.' This statement reflects what I have called Sartre's 'hard-line' position on responsibility: people are responsible for what they are; they, in effect, *choose* to be what they are. As we saw when we looked at *No Exit*, he has no truck with excuses, with people denying that they are not who they want to be. Everyone, according to Sartre, is totally responsible for who they are. Hence, they choose themselves.

Although Sartre continues as if he is just drawing out the implications of this claim, in fact he makes a very different point when he says that, in choosing oneself, one also chooses *for everyone*. Not only is this claim different from the first one, it also appears to undercut the stress on individuality that is so characteristic of Existentialism. Didn't the Existentialists intend to create a philosophical point of view that opposed the conformist tendencies that they saw as undermining people's ability to live their lives fully and freely? How can we square this point of view with Sartre's claim that my choices don't just represent decisions I am making about how to live my own individual life but also my decisions for humanity as a whole?

A more promising attempt to resolve the problem of the authentic tyrant is made by Simone de Beauvoir (see text box opposite) in her book, *The Ethics of Ambiguity*. The ambiguity that de Beauvoir refers to is that between the in-itself and the for-itself, facticity and transcendence, or, as she puts it, the fact that each human being is 'still a part of this world of which he is a consciousness.' The problem confronting her is how to develop an ethics in the face of the ambiguous situation she thinks characterizes our existence. The answer that she proposes relies on the fact that 'every man needs the freedom of other men and, in a sense, always wants it, even though he may be a tyrant' (*The Ethics of Ambiguity*, 70). This is a difficult claim to understand. The justification that de Beauvoir gives for it is that '[o]nly the freedom of others keeps each one of us from hardening in the absurdity of facticity' (*The Ethics of Ambiguity*, 71). De Beauvoir thinks that other people keep us alive to our own nature as transcendent beings and that, without their input, we would be unable to maintain that flexibility indicative of the for-itself. We'll look more closely at her justification in a moment. For now, we will merely note that she explains why she thinks that we need to respect the freedom of others, for '[t]o will oneself free is also to will others free' (*The Ethics of Ambiguity*, 73).

Simone de Beauvoir (1908–1986) is one of the central figures in the Existentialist Movement in post-World War II France. Her writings were voluminous and varied. She wrote many semi-autobiographical novels, such as *The Mandarins* (1954), which give the reader a good sense of what the day-to-day lives of the Existentialists were like. Her philosophical writings include *The Ethics of Ambiguity* (1947), an attempt to ground an ethical theory on Existentialist principles; *The Second Sex* (1949), a revolutionary treatise on the oppression of women; and *The Coming of Age* (1970), another innovative work that brought the process of aging to public attention.

De Beauvoir is also known because of her life-long association with Sartre, which began when they were students. Although de Beauvoir was quite deferential to Sartre in her accounts of their roles in the development of Existentialism, recent feminist scholars have argued that she made a greater contribution to it than is generally acknowledged. According to them, many of Sartre's ideas had their origins in de Beauvoir's writings, specifically her short stories and novels. Whatever the truth of this claim, she deserves to be taken more seriously as an original thinker in the Existentialist Tradition than she has often been.

De Beauvoir claims, then, that a person who wishes to live as a free being must respect the freedom of others. A first thing to note is that this view departs from Sartre's claim that, in acting, a free person legislates how everyone should act. De Beauvoir keeps the focus on the individual, asserting that a free individual needs to respect the individuality of others. As we shall see in the next chapter, this view supports the Existentialists' political program of working for the freedom of all.

For now, however, we need to consider whether de Beauvoir's view provides a solution to the problem of the authentic tyrant that I raised through the example of Hitler. In fact, the answer is apparent: although Hitler might think that he was being authentic by exterminating the Jews, de Beauvoir would say that he was not, because his racist policies refused to support the freedom of other human beings. What we need to ask is why she thinks that a person's freedom requires her to respect and support the freedom of others.

De Beauvoir's answer is that, without other such beings with whom to interact, a person will fall into facticity, be no more than a 'thing.' In making this claim, de Beauvoir draws on the Existentialists' claim that the self–other relationship is as basic to humans as the self–object one. Not only do we inhabit a world not of our own making, but it is a world that contains other beings, other consciousnesses, who are just like us. To attain freedom, we need not only to choose ourselves, to make our own being, we need to do so in relation to others who are themselves free beings. If we do not act so as to foster their freedom, according to de Beauvoir, we jeopardize our own freedom as well.

This is a difficult argument whose complete exposition would demand a more full discussion. Still, its basic thought seems apparent: because we humans are social beings, we need to interact with others whose freedom we support in order for us to truly be free. The tyrant who thinks he is free is not, for the course of action he has chosen – one in which he oppresses others – is one that requires him to constantly reinforce his decision. But, in acting this way, he contradicts his own nature as a free being. So, once Hitler chose to eliminate the Jews, he was forced to rigidly continue with that policy, for it provoked enmity and opposition, and not just from those who were immediately affected by it. Because being free requires us to maintain our stance as nihilating beings, and because this requires that we not accept any rigid definition of our selves, we have to act in ways that foster not only our own freedom, but also the freedom of everyone else. Although this is not in itself completely convincing as a refutation of the problem of the authentic tyrant, it does point to an interesting line of argumentation that might do the trick.

In attempting to defend Existentialism from the charge that it cannot ground an acceptable ethics, de Beauvoir moves from the realm of the individual into the domain of the social. Despite the claim often made against the Existentialists that their theory was inherently individualistic, we can already see from de Beauvoir's account of ethics that this is not completely true. In the next chapter, we will explore the Existentialists' account of the social world – and, in particular, of social oppression – in more detail.

8

Oppression

In previous chapters, we have seen that the Existentialists take a very dim view of bourgeois society. As early as the mid-nineteenth century, Kierkegaard had excoriated his fellow citizens for their conformism, their lack of individuality. And this chord continued to be struck by all subsequent Existentialists. They all see people living lives determined by their fears and anxieties, lives that failed to meet the standard of bold if pessimistic individualism that the Existentialists endorsed.

An obvious question to ask is why so many people succumb to the conformism that the Existentialists despise. We explored one part of the answer in the last chapter: Fear of death leads many to accept the tranquilizing life available as part of a They, with its strategies for avoiding the onset of metaphysical anxiety. But there is a very important supplement to this explanation for the prevalence of social conformity that the Existentialists also develop: they see modern society as permeated by structures of social oppression that enforce conformity and keep people from becoming the free individuals they have the potential to be.

In discussing the Existentialists' theory of social oppression, I will focus on the writings of Sartre, de Beauvoir, and Frantz Fanon, all of whom lived in post-World War II France. At that time, French society was implicated in at least three different forms of oppression analyzed by these thinkers: anti-Semitic racism (Sartre), sexism (de Beauvoir), and colonialism (Fanon). As we shall see, these analyses of oppression are significant because of the way each applies elements of the account of being human we have already explored to the phenomenon of societal oppression. The unique feature of the Existentialist approach to analyzing oppression is its tracing it back to fundamental facets of our experience as humans.

It is worth emphasizing that the Existentialists' concern with oppression is no mere after-thought to a theory that has no inherently social character. Indeed, Existentialism, at least in its French version, is a deeply politically engaged philosophy whose adherents manifest a real concern with helping to eliminate the oppressive structures that keep human beings enslaved, even in our modern, highly technological world. Sartre remains the paradigm of the engaged intellectual, one who used the renown he had received from his writings to advocate for the political causes he endorsed. And he was not alone in this committed stance. His fellow Existentialists – Maurice Merleau-Ponty (see text box overleaf), Simone de Beauvoir, Albert Camus, and Frantz Fanon – all agreed with Sartre that philosophy had to be engaged in contemporary life and not, as Hegel had said, only with lifeforms that had already been transcended. In their view, the owl of Minerva, Hegel's metaphor for philosophy, had to get used to flying in daylight. In this respect, they agreed with Marx's claim that philosophy should not only attempt to interpret the world but also – and even more importantly – seek to transform it.

Anti-Semitism

Although Sartre wrote many political essays dealing with contemporary issues, *Anti-Semite and Jew* (1946) was his first comprehensive attempt to use the framework of Existentialism to comprehend a form of social oppression. The received attitude toward anti-Semitism at the time was that it was the result of the anti-Semites' false beliefs about Jews. From this point of view, the phenomenon of anti-Semitism was based on the anti-Semites' ignorance about Jews. Still today, many people think of racism as a set of mistaken ideas that racists have about

Maurice Merleau-Ponty (1908–1961) was a pivotal figure in post-World War II French Existentialism. Together with Sartre and de Beauvoir, he founded *Les Temps Modernes*, the central journal of the Existentialist Movement. Unlike his fellow Parisian Existentialists, he was a university professor and held the Chair of Philosophy at the College de France until his untimely death from a stroke.

Of all the Existentialist thinkers, Merleau-Ponty was the only one who was favorably disposed to science. All of his philosophical writings – most centrally *Phenomenology of Perception* (1945) – are an attempt to undermine the mind–body dualism so prevalent in Western thought since Descartes. In its place, Merleau-Ponty advocated a monistic conception of a body-subject, in which both 'mental' and 'physical' attributes are closely intertwined. He was also very interested in the psycho-physical process of perception and used the latest experimental results to undermine the traditional view that the process of perception depends on discrete sense-data.

Like the other Existentialists, Merleau-Ponty was deeply politically engaged. When he criticized Sartre for his sympathy with the Communist Party, the two had a highly publicized 'break.' Although Merleau-Ponty had earlier been sympathetic to Marxism, he came to believe that the Korean War established that the Soviet Union was a totalitarian state.

people of other races. What this suggests is that racism, in all of its various different forms, can be eliminated by providing people with accurate information about the oppressed. You could thus 'fix' the anti-Semite by explaining that, for example, not all Jews have big noses nor are they all obsessed with money.

It is clear that this view of 'anti-Semitism as ignorance' is completely inadequate as an explanation. While the anti-Semite may be ignorant about many features of Jewish culture, this cannot explain why she favors the oppression of Jews. After all, having false beliefs about a social group does not necessarily produce a negative socio-political attitude, much less a program of oppression. I know very little about the Inuit, for example, but think they deserve the same respect due any human being. A more sophisticated explanation is required of this form of persecution.

Sartre attempts to provide a more adequate explanation of anti-Semitism by drawing on some of the key ideas of Existentialism. He begins by claiming that it is an orientation to the world: 'Anti-Semitism is a free and total choice of oneself, a comprehensive attitude that one adopts not only toward Jews but toward men in general, toward history and society; it is at one and the same time a passion and a conception of the world' (*Anti-Semite and Jew*, 17). Here, Sartre treats anti-Semitism as more than a lack, something other than simply 'ignorance.' Rather, he sees it as an affirmative stance that a person has chosen, and one that is not limited just to Jews. Anti-Semitism, Sartre says, is a basic orientation that a person has toward the world. Using the Existentialist notion that people make free choices about who they are, Sartre posits anti-Semitism as the result of a fundamental choice that the anti-Semite makes about her relationship to society and other people in general.

Still, this does not explain why the anti-Semite targets Jews. To begin to explain this, Sartre employs the important Existentialist thesis that humans have an ambivalent attitude toward their own freedom. He claims that anti-Semitism results from the anti-Semite's fear of her own freedom:

[The anti-Semite] chooses the irremediable out of fear of being free; he chooses mediocrity out of fear of being alone, and out of pride he makes of this irremediable mediocrity a rigid aristocracy. To this end he finds the existence of the Jew absolutely necessary. Otherwise to whom would he be superior? ... Thus the anti-Semite is in the unhappy position of having a vital need for the very enemy he wishes to destroy. (*Anti-Semite and Jew*, 27–8)

Sartre here posits anti-Semitism as a form of Bad Faith. Someone exhibits Bad Faith, you will recall, when they somehow deny their fundamental freedom as a human being. According to Sartre, this is just what the anti-Semite does. First, she chooses mediocrity. That is to say, the anti-Semite, like many others, conforms to a set of norms in order to be part of a social group, a They. The benefit of so doing is to feel part of a group and to fend off the anguish that comes from acknowledging one's freedom and responsibility. What we have not yet emphasized is the Existentialist claim that those who accept the dictates of a They also accept what Sartre here calls 'mediocrity.' Because all the members of a group have to fulfill the standards of conduct it imposes, exceptionality is ruled out. All must be mediocre in order to ensure the social uniformity that constitutes the They. However, Sartre goes on to claim, the anti-Semite is not comfortable with acknowledging her own acceptance of such leveling norms and so needs to find a way to see herself as superior. And this is precisely where the Jews come in: the anti-Semite's efforts at Bad Faith succeed because she has the Jew to feel superior to.

There are a number of interesting features of this Existentialist analysis of anti-Semitism. First, because Sartre's analysis places anti-Semitism into the general category of Bad Faith, it shows that what appeared to be a theory of an individual's behavior – Bad Faith – actually is useful for understanding social phenomena. The importance of this is that, aside from providing insight into the nature of anti-Semitism itself, Sartre's Bad Faith-based theory provides a general framework for developing an Existentialist understanding of societal oppression. In a moment, we will see how other Existentialist theorists applied Sartre's insights to the phenomena of sexism and colonialism.

Sartre's analysis also shows why it is a mistake to treat anti-Semitism as simply the result of ignorance on the part of the anti-Semite. Mobilizing the Existentialist notion of a situation as well as the view of humans as ambivalent about their own freedom, Sartre is able to see anti-Semitism as a response that the anti-Semite makes to her own situation as a finite human being. The ignorant stereotypes that the anti-Semite employs are not by themselves adequate to ground this mode of social oppression. Rather, once the denigration of the Jews has acquired its metaphysical foundation via the anti-Semite's attempt to deny her own choice of mediocrity, such images as that of the big-nosed Jew function to confirm the already posited inferiority of the Jew. Thus, as a result, Sartre's analysis shows why anti-Semitism cannot be combated simply by giving people more information, as if it were just an epistemological problem. The anti-Semite's 'ignorance' about Jews is actually a substantive phenomenon having its roots in the anti-Semite's need to obscure her own Bad Faith.

Sartre also points out that the anti-Semite is in a very curious position. Two important aspects of anti-Semitism are its hatred of Jews and its desire to eliminate them from society. But, at the same time, Sartre claims, the anti-Semite needs the Jew, for without the presence of the Jew there would be no one whom the anti-Semite could use to secure her sense of her own superiority. That is, the Jew represents the *solution* to the anti-Semite's *problem* and, without him, that problem would remain unresolved. The anti-Semite, faced with her own choice to join a They, *creates* the Jew as a way of avoiding knowledge of what she has done and also of establishing the superiority of this 'They' or group. Without the Jew, she would be forced to either invent a replacement or face her own life without this strategy of denial. So the anti-Semite is dependent upon the very being she purports to hate and wish to eliminate.

In making this part of his argument, Sartre is creatively applying an important Hegelian thesis. In his famous analysis of lordship-and-bondage in the *Phenomenology of Mind*, Hegel argues that the lord, who enslaves the bondsman in order to gain confirmation of his own independence as a conscious being, winds up dependent upon the bondsman, for the latter is necessary in order for the lord to feel independent. This ironic reversal is characteristic of what Hegel calls 'the dialectical nature of reality': things that initially appear to be structured in one way turn out, upon deeper analysis, to be the exact opposite, as when the supposedly independent being turns out to really be the dependent one. Sartre's use of this idea reiterates a lesson we have already learned: that Hegel, whom we encountered as the foe taken on by the Existentialists for his embrace of the rationality of reality, is also an important source of Existentialist theories. Although they have many quarrels with him, the Existentialists also find inspiration in many of Hegel's analyses of the nature of human existence. Indeed, he, more than any previous philosopher, took the full range of human experience as the appropriate subject for philosophical analysis, treating human existence as involving difficult and even tragic philosophical choices. So even when they disagree with some of his more specific claims, the Existentialists remain indebted to Hegel for his perceptive account of the struggles of human life.

It is worth pointing out that there is an element of contingency in Sartre's account. Given the dynamics of anti-Semitic Bad Faith, the anti-Semite needs to have some group to which she can feel superior. The Jews are a suitable group for this role because European culture already contained anti-Semitic ideas and images that dated all the way back, in some cases, to the stories of Jesus' crucifixion. What this makes clear is that *modern* anti-Semitism – the real object of Sartre's analysis – has its roots in the traditional anti-Semitism of Christian culture itself.

Gender oppression

One of the most prescient and insightful uses of Existentialism as a tool for social and political analysis was put forward by Simone de Beauvoir in her path-breaking book, *The Second Sex*, published in 1949. Emerging seemingly from a theoretical vacuum, *The Second Sex* used the tools of Existentialism to explore the nature of sexism or gender oppression.

'One is not born, but rather becomes, a woman' (*The Second Sex*, 301). With this bold pronouncement, de Beauvoir announces the guiding thesis of her analysis of gender oppression: being a woman is a matter of following socially determined patterns of behavior rather than a biological fact. To see what she means, it will be useful to distinguish sex and gender. 'Sex' refers to the biological facts that sort human beings into two predominant groups, biological males and biological females, although there are other sexes besides these two dominant ones. 'Gender,' on the other hand, refers to the social roles of masculinity and femininity. De Beauvoir's thesis is that femininity, the gender role that is characteristic of 'woman,' is learned, not something inherent in biological females. We should note, though, that de Beauvoir does not herself make this verbal distinction between sex and gender, so that we will have to be careful in interpreting her claims to determine whether she is referring to a biological or social fact.

How, then, are we to understand the social roles into which people are placed according to their gender? De Beauvoir claims that we need to understand 'woman' as the negation of 'man,' which is the primary or 'valorized' term. To be human is, implicitly, to be a man; to be a woman is, inherently, to be inferior.

> Thus humanity is male and man defines woman not in herself but as relative to him; she is not regarded as an autonomous being ... She is defined and differentiated with reference to man and not he with reference to her; she is the incidental, the inessential as opposed to the essential. He is the Subject, he is the Absolute – she is the Other. (*The Second Sex*, xviii–xix)

De Beauvoir takes herself here to be describing, in ontological terms, the nature of the man–woman relationship. She asserts that man is always the dominant term in the relationship and woman, always the subordinate, the one that is forced to conceive of herself not on her own terms but in relation to the other.

From there, De Beauvoir's analysis continues along similar lines to Sartre's claims about anti–Semitism. She argues that men, especially those who feel inferior to other men, benefit from gender oppression because it gives them a way of affirming their worth, that is, by allowing them to feel superior to women. This is the rationale for gender domination: men, when forced to acknowledge their inferiority to other men, are able to maintain their self-confidence and self-assurance by maintaining their dominance over women. In *The Second Sex*, de Beauvoir traces out in great detail various different forms such male domination of women has taken. In doing so, she discusses historical, biological, and cultural views of women's situation. Thus, while employing the abstract theory derived from Existentialism, de Beauvoir fills it out with a wealth of empirical detail that is often missing from the more ahistorical works of other Existentialist thinkers. And it is in these more detailed accounts that de Beauvoir's analysis exhibits its compelling power.

Still, there is a theoretical question that de Beauvoir herself finds pressing: why do women accept their relegation to a position subordinate to men? Her reply involves one of the most controversial aspects of her analysis of gender oppression. De Beauvoir begins by noting that women are in a very different situation from other oppressed social groups such as Jews or Blacks (*Nègre*). Unlike people in those groups, women joined to men in what de Beauvoir calls, adopting Heidegger's terminology, a *Mitsein* (literally, being-with or, more colloquially, joint-existence). Her point is that men and women are connected to one another by a necessary tie. One obvious reason is that the propagation of the human race depends on their union. Jews or Blacks, although tied to their oppressors, can seek to liberate themselves from them. There is no reason why they need to interact. But women need men in order to continue the propagation of the human race. As a result, their situation is different from that of other oppressed groups, for they cannot simply live in isolation from their oppressor.

Another possible ground for thinking that women cannot sever their connection to men is that the object of many women's sexual desire is male. Whether de Beauvoir would agree that human sexuality necessitates such a connection is unclear, particularly in view of her own bisexuality. Nonetheless, she claims that the liberation of women needs to follow a different path from that of Jews or Blacks, for that liberation cannot completely sever the man–woman bond, no matter how fundamentally it might aim to transform it.

The most controversial aspect of de Beauvoir's analysis of women's oppression, however, lies in her claim that women choose to accept their dependent status. Contentious as this claim is, it is characteristic of the Existentialist perspective and allows us to see an important aspect of gender oppression that other, less frank analyses obscure. De Beauvoir points to the general human tendency to forgo freedom and aspire to a more thing-like status that allows people to evade many of the difficulties that freedom strews in their path. De Beauvoir asserts that women have accepted their oppression by men not primarily because it has provided them with economic security – although she acknowledges that also plays a role – but because their oppression has provided women with the *metaphysical solace* of avoiding the burden of freedom.

In order to understand de Beauvoir's view, we need to make reference to a dichotomy touched on earlier. You will recall that the Existentialists emphasized the human capacity to move beyond one's given situation. This capacity they called 'transcendence' and all that limited it 'immanence.' De Beauvoir applies this dichotomy to the situation of women: because they are consigned by men to the realm of immanence, women are 'spared' the travails of transcendence. Women are 'freed' from the burden of their own freedom, saved from having to face all the difficult and painful questions about life that confront those pursuing transcendence – generally men, according to de Beauvoir (speaking about the society she was living in), except for a few, exceptional women. Because they are relegated to immanent activities – making meals, cleaning the house, and so on – women, like the Grand Inquisitor's subjects, receive security in exchange for giving up their freedom as human beings.

Subsequent feminists have pointed out that de Beauvoir, not a mother herself, gives short shrift to the raising of the next generation. For them, this task, although traditionally undervalued, is crucial, indeed, it is one in which women can realize their transcendence. Perhaps because of her own personal situation, de Beauvoir failed to give adequate weight to this activity in her analysis of women's situation.

De Beauvoir's analysis of gender oppression also makes clear what she believes would be needed for its abolition. It is not merely a matter of achieving economic equality, although she recognizes that this is an important prerequisite for gender equality, for the structure of gender oppression has Existential as well as economic roots. In order for women to be truly liberated from gender oppression, there would have to be a more general social transformation that would undermine the assumption that 'woman is the other of man,' that men are inherently superior to women. So, female human beings would have to be acknowledged to be the equal of male human beings in every domain, and this would require a change not just in women, but in men as well.

Subsequent generations of feminists have taken inspiration from de Beauvoir's ground-breaking analysis of gender oppression. Although they have argued with many of her specific claims, there is general agreement that the Existentialist perspective she uses to illuminate sexism as a pervasive and highly detrimental social phenomenon paved the way for all future analyses of it.

Colonialism

The final example of how Existentialism can illuminate the nature of societal oppression involves *colonialism*. *Wikipedia* defines colonialism as 'the extension of a nation's sovereignty over territory beyond its borders by the establishment of either settler colonies or administrative dependencies in which indigenous populations are directly ruled or displaced.' The form of colonialism that we will be discussing is one in which the indigenous peoples are ruled by members of the colonialist society, which takes itself to have authority over the colonized people. As in other relationships of social oppression, there is an economic basis to colonialism, for the colonizing society is able to exploit the colonized society to gain material advantages for itself. Thus, in the seventeenth and eighteenth centuries, different European nations colonized the Americas in order to benefit from the vast natural resources that had been discovered there. Still, from the Existentialist point of view, there is more to colonialism than its economic structure. As with the other forms that social oppression takes, the Existentialists see the roots of colonialism to lie in the dynamics of our experience as finite creatures.

Frantz Fanon (see text box overleaf) extended the perspective of Existentialism to the phenomenon of colonialism in his book, *Black Skin, White Masks*. Unlike Sartre's analysis of anti-Jewish racism and de Beauvoir's analysis of gender oppression – both of which take as their fundamental theoretical tool the notion of

Bad Faith – Fanon's analysis of colonialism relies on Sartre's theory of 'the look' to theorize the colonialist oppression of Blacks. As we have seen, Sartre claimed that humans acquire an alienated understanding of themselves when they are looked at (or, at least, imagine that they are) by an other. The resulting self contains an alienated self-understanding because it posits one as possessing a determinate nature – such as, to recall Sartre's example, that of a jealous lover – that obscures the nihilating potentialities of the self.

Frantz Fanon (1925–1961) was not a professional philosopher. Born in the French colony of Martinique in the Caribbean, Fanon later moved to France where he worked as a psychiatrist. In his later years, he moved to Algeria, whose anti-colonial movement he supported. Eventually, he became a politician and even served as an ambassador for the Algerian Provisional Government.

Fanon is best known for two books. The first, *Black Skin, White Masks* (1952), analyzes the situation of the post-colonial subject, detailing a variety of ways in which colonialism dehumanizes those it rules. It employs an Existentialist framework to explore the alienation of the Black man and the possibilities for his achieving an authentic existence. His second book, *The Wretched of the Earth* (1961), extends Fanon's analysis of colonization and focuses on the political process of decolonization. Unlike traditional Marxist theory that privileged the revolutionary potential of the (male) working class, Fanon saw the African peasantry as a potential agent of political liberation.

Fanon's influence extended well beyond academic circles, though he has also been influential in them, especially in the discipline of cultural studies. His ideas were picked up by many of the leaders of the anti-imperialist struggles following the Algerian War, including Steve Biko and Ernesto Che Guevara. He is the subject of a fascinating film, *Frantz Fanon: Black Skin, White Mask*, made by Isaac Julien.

This theory provides the key to Fanon's understanding of his experience as what is now called 'a colonial subject,' that is, someone who was native to a non-Western society but was brought up within the circumstances of colonization. Just as Sartre introduced his conception of the alienated self through a phenomenological investigation of jealousy, Fanon similarly traces an experience that gives rise to 'the colonialist self.' His discussion, however, is avowedly autobiographical. He considers what happened when someone – in the story he tells, it is a young boy speaking in fear to his mother – looked at him and said, 'Look, a Negro!' Here is how Fanon summarizes his experience:

> I came into the world imbued with the will to find a meaning in things, my spirit filled with the desire to attain to the source of the world, and then I found that I was an object in the midst of other objects. (*Black Skin, White Masks*, 109)

Fanon's description of his experience here parallels Sartre's of the jealous man in *Being and Nothingness*. Fanon attributes to himself a consciousness that is probably best described as philosophical, for he says that he was interested in comprehending the nature of the world in which he found himself. But a child's exclamation *stole* that self from him because, by asking his mother to *look*, the child posited Fanon as someone whose nature could be revealed simply by a glance. Because the child was able to 'capture' Fanon's nature simply by looking at him, his glance turned Fanon into an object, that is, the object seen by the child. We have seen that the Existentialists distinguish sharply between the being of physical objects and that of humans. The former – varying from tables to trees – have a nature which observation can reveal. Human beings, though, are different. As nihilating beings, we do not have a predetermined nature that can be read off our appearance. When a person is able to 'see' who one is, her seeing actually results in one's objectification. This is what happened to Fanon. The colonialist child constitutes Fanon as a colonial subject with a completely *legible* nature by reading it off his appearance.

Having employed Sartre's analysis of 'the look' to good effect in explaining the genesis of the colonial subject as an objectified being, Fanon goes on to argue that the legibility of the Black man distinguishes his situation from that of the Jew. Because the Jew is white, he can remain 'unknown in his Jewishness' (*Black Skin, White Masks*, 115). That is, the Jew's white skin allows him to be invisible, at least some of the time, for a Jew cannot always be recognized by his skin color. Indeed, there are many Jews who do not 'look' Jewish. In fact, my mother, who was Jewish and who grew up in Germany during the rise of National Socialism, was blond and had blue eyes. She didn't 'look' Jewish. Because people took her to be a gentile, they did not hide their anti-Semitic attitudes and she overheard many anti-Semitic conversations. But Fanon thinks this cannot happen in the case of Blacks, for he takes their Blackness to be registered on their skins.

In recent times, this claim has been disputed. The philosopher and artist Adrian Piper, for example, has provocatively challenged the idea that Blackness is visible. Because many people take her light skin color to indicate that she is white, Piper views Blackness as just as capable of 'unknownness' as Fanon claims Jewishness to be. But even if we dispute the claim that legibility is a necessary feature of the colonization of Blacks, we can agree that many Blacks do have to contend with it in just the way Fanon describes.

Among the consequences of his legibility, Fanon claims, was a general failure to acknowledge him simply as an individual in terms of his accomplishments: 'It was always the *Negro* teacher, the *Negro* doctor' (*Black Skin, White Masks*, 117). His point here, one that has echoes in analogous claims made by contemporary feminists, is that his black skin means that his accomplishments are never seen as those of a human being, but always of a *Black* man. Even if the colonialist attitude is not expressed as bluntly as it was by the young child who saw Fanon as a Negro, it is repeatedly reinforced when people use the term 'Negro' to qualify his accomplishments and positions, leading Fanon to feel that his own individuality was routinely passed over.

The task of overcoming his alienated identity as a Black colonial subject is a difficult one for Fanon. He realizes that his identity has been completely constructed by the colonial powers through their practice of 'cultural imposition' in which young Black children in the colonies are taught to read the literature of the colonizer. As a result, the young internalize the colonists' values, which emphasize the inferiority of the colonized, thereby even further increasing their alienation from their nature as fully human.

The Négritude Movement was a literary and political movement that began in the 1930s among intellectuals in the French colonies that provided Fanon with a means of developing what he calls a 'disalienated' self. It sought to develop a transnational identity among all the native peoples in the French colonies, one that would transcend their individual national identities. For Fanon, this represented a way of conceptualizing his Blackness that did not come from 'the other,' as it had when he was the object of the look of the young child. Through poems, literature, and other writings, the Négritude Movement created a sense of disalienated Black identity. In valorizing this sense of Blackness, Fanon employed the ideas of Existentialism. For example, he embraced the antidualistic thinking advocated by the Existentialists – most centrally Maurice Merleau-Ponty – according to which the human being must be conceived of as an embodied-mind and not the mental substance attached to a body of the Cartesian tradition.

> Yes, we are – we Negroes – backward, simple, free in our behavior. That is because for us the body is not something opposed to what you call the mind. We are in the world. And long live the couple, Man and Earth! (*Black Skin, White Masks*, 127)

Fanon sees in the Negro the possibility of a nonalienated form of human existence that corresponds more closely to what the Existentialists claim is the real nature of human existence than do the forms of white existence described by the Western tradition.

So it is not surprising to find Fanon deeply shocked by Sartre's assertion that the Négritude Movement creates a consciousness of Black identity that needs to be transcended and replaced by a more universal consciousness that he associates with Marxism. Here is what Sartre says: 'Négritude appears as the minor term in a dialectical progression ... Négritude is the root of its own destruction, it is a transition and not a conclusion, a means and not an ultimate end' (quoted, *Black Skin, White Masks*, 130). The reason that Négritude is only a transitional state of consciousness for Sartre is that, at the time that he made the assessment, he accepted a Marxist point of view in which racial (and gender) oppression were but expressions of the more basic form of oppression, class oppression or economic exploitation. But, anticipating more contemporary critiques of traditional Marxism, Fanon refuses to see colonial racist oppression as subordinate to class oppression. For him as a Black colonial subject, anti-Black racism is the *primary* form of oppression and he upbraids Sartre for failing to understand its significance for colonial subjects:

> At the very moment when I was trying to grasp my own being, Sartre, who remained The Other, gave me a name and thus shattered my last illusion ... Jean-Paul Sartre had forgotten that the Negro suffers in his body quite differently than the white man. (*Black Skin, White Masks*, 138)

Fanon here rebukes Sartre for remaining within the logic of colonialist thinking, thereby attempting to reinscribe Fanon's Blackness into a schema that is familiar to him, Sartre, but that once more places Fanon in the role of the Negro seen by a white. In his 'quest for disalienation by a doctor of medicine born in Guadeloupe,' Fanon sees the development of a Black identity through the Négritude Movement as crucial and necessary (*Black Skin, White Masks*, 223).

So, Fanon employs the conceptual framework and tools provided by Existentialism in order to develop an account of colonial oppression as well as an understanding of the means for its transcendence. As in Sartre's analysis of anti-Semitism and de Beauvoir's of gender oppression, Existentialism provides an important theoretical perspective for understanding and criticizing colonial oppression. Because of its view of the human being as a free, nihilating consciousness and its emphasis on humans' ambivalence about their own freedom, Existentialism provides a unique lens for viewing the nature of social oppression, one that emphasizes that oppression, as a human phenomenon, must have an experiential or Existential dimension that has often been overlooked by theorists employing other theoretical perspectives.

The personal is philosophical

Before leaving the topic of Existentialism and oppression, I want to discuss one other way in which the Existentialists attempted to free human beings from oppressive social arrangements. What I have in mind is the personal commitment that Sartre and de Beauvoir made to live their lives in a very public way free of the intimidating constraints of bourgeois morality.

Many writers and philosophers have condemned bourgeois or 'middle class' morality. George Bernard Shaw's play *Pygmalion*, for example, contains a spirited attack on the hypocrisy of such a moral outlook. Bourgeois morality consists of a set of norms for regulating human social interactions that resulted from the decline of the aristocracy with the rise of capitalism. Among the reasons that have been suggested for its development is the role that it purportedly plays in modern industrial life, for people need to have a character structure that will allow them to take their required place in the processes of capitalist production.

There are a variety of different grounds for criticizing these norms that point to distinct ways in which they constrain human beings. Here, I only want to reiterate de Beauvoir's Existentialist assertion that marriage, one of the lynch pins of bourgeois morality, reinscribes the subordinate position of women in society into that miniature of society that is the family. Within the family, women are condemned to immanence and men are given the opportunity to achieve transcendence. Although, according to de Beauvoir, bearing children seals women's fate, she claimed that marriage alone was sufficient to consign women to their fate as the mistresses of immanence.

The Existentialist perspective that Sartre and de Beauvoir shared gave them a healthy contempt for bourgeois morality, which they saw as founded on a denial of the real nature of human beings. As a result, they saw marriage as a bourgeois institution that enslaves women. But they did not just formulate theoretical criticisms of this – and other – bourgeois social institutions, they also chose to live their lives in a way that flaunted their contempt for marriage and bourgeois morality in general, and this made Existentialism not just a philosophical perspective but a highly controversial lived one. It also established the two philosophers as role models for many in the 1950s who felt the demands of social conformity to be unacceptable.

In 1929, Sartre and de Beauvoir had formed a romantic liaison as students studying for their *agrégation*, an important examination in France that would determine their academic futures. At this time, they realized that they had a very special relationship, one that was founded on their intellectual compatibility. But they chose not to follow the usual course of action and marry, for they saw marriage as a contract that limited the freedom of both the partners. So, they made an agreement of commitment to each other, an agreement that allowed each of them to pursue other sexual relationships. Their understanding was that those affairs would not undermine their fundamental commitment to each other. Theirs was, as de Beauvoir said of it, an 'essential love' that could admit 'contingent' affairs. In our post-sexual revolution world, it is hard to imagine both the daring of this agreement and its scandalous reception. Although it was relatively common for men in France at the time to have affairs, it was much less frequent for women to do so and certainly, when they did, they were not as public about it as de Beauvoir was. Her contract with Sartre struck a deep blow against the dominance of social convention in favor of less restrictive practices, even though it scandalized the public, who still retained a sense of bourgeois propriety. So, de Beauvoir and Sartre attempted to live their lives so as to very publicly embody the values they stood for philosophically.

Existentialism, then, has a unique take on the phenomenon of social oppression. Because of its emphasis on the dynamics of human experience, the Existentialists approach oppression as a phenomenon to be explained in terms of the fundamental categories of human life. And this resulted in important insights into the nature of anti-Semitic racism, sexism, and colonialism. But it also led to the Existentialists personalizing their theories. Their own lives were shaped by their commitment to undercut oppression and realize the freedom they took to be available to all humans in no matter what circumstances.

9

Conclusion

Our guided tour of Existentialism is almost at an end. But before it is, I want to take a moment to assess the general perspective of Existentialism, to ask whether this form of philosophical thinking really deserves our endorsement.

In the previous chapters, I have generally eschewed criticizing the theories and claims of the Existentialists. I did this because I wanted to develop a comprehensive account of their different theories and points of view prior to asking whether they are valid. But now that we have a good overview of Existentialism as a whole, it is time to consider some of the most significant criticisms that have been leveled at this philosophical school.

The Existentialists' manner of philosophizing has often been critiqued as being too subjective, too firmly rooted in the experience of individuals. As we have seen, the Existentialists do focus on people's experience, but that is because they believe that other philosophical methods have led to a *reified* conception of the human being, one that treats us as if we were more similar to other things in the world than we really are. By focusing in sometimes minute detail on the nature of our experience as embodied, thinking beings, with a finite life span, the Existentialists hoped to free us from all such distorted and inadequate accounts of our own nature.

But some philosophers have held that this approach fails to take seriously enough the *social* nature of human existence. Jürgen Habermas (1929–), for example, rejects any philosophical point of view that depends on what he views as the outmoded stance of a 'philosophy of the subject.' Philosophy needs to begin, he asserts, with the recognition that human beings are inherently social beings whose interactions with one another need to be theoretically acknowledged at the most basic level. There is simply no level at which human beings exist outside of, and apart from, their interactions with others. From his point of view, the Existentialists' own starting point is inadequate because it is too subjective, too individualistic.

This is not the place for a complete discussion of this criticism of Existentialism. However, we can note that, despite the Existentialists' emphasis on the individual and its uniqueness, they do acknowledge the social nature of the human being. Both Heidegger and Sartre, to limit my discussion to these important thinkers, conceive of human beings as having an essential tie to others. Heidegger conceptualizes this as 'joint existence' (*Mitsein*, 'being-with'), while Sartre posits 'being-for-others' as a fundamental aspect of the ontology of 'human reality.' To dismiss Existentialism for its subjectivist point of view thus seems wrong-headed, for the Existentialists were among the first to acknowledge, emphasize, and theoretically register the social nature of human beings.

Still, it may be that the Existentialists have not incorporated one of their own basic insights as fully as necessary into their conceptions of all the different domains of human existence. For example, their theory of language may still be too individualistic in its orientation, failing to emphasize adequately the role that language plays in the transmission of culture from one generation to another. But such a failing, if indeed it is one, should be taken as a call for further development of an Existential theory of language rather than a blanket dismissal of this philosophical point of view.

Existentialism has also often been criticized for its ahistorical perspective. In fact, I have quietly smuggled this criticism into my presentation when I discussed how the Existentialists took as part of the human condition features of human life that were results of that broad social development known as 'modernity,' as if there was a basic human condition that inhered in every society and in every historical epoch. Many philosophers object to this idea, for they claim that, at the most basic level, the lives of human beings register the historical and social circumstances in which they live. According to these philosophers, there is no 'human condition,' if what is meant by that phrase is a set of basic issues or concerns that face human beings no matter what the socio-historical context of their existence.

This criticism is allied to another: that Existentialism has a Eurocentric bias. Take the notion that there is an authentic attitude toward death that a human being can have, one in which death is viewed as the final and total end of a person's existence. Doesn't this theory embody a Western view of death, one that stands opposed to views of death-and-life as a recurrent cycle such as embodied in Buddhism? And isn't such a privileging of Western views of human life inherent in a great deal of Existentialist theorizing?

But even if there are aspects of Existential thought that are Eurocentric, there are others that are not. For example, consider Fanon's analysis of colonialism, deeply rooted in Existentialist theory. The Existentialists would point to Fanon's analysis to show that, not only are their theories not Eurocentric, but they are actually helpful in illuminating the structures and experiences of other places and cultures. Indeed, from their own point of view, Existentialism should be acknowledged as one of the least Eurocentric of any Western philosophical theory or school. Although this is hardly a fully satisfactory response to this objection, it does show that Existentialism has played an important role in the development of a non-Eurocentric philosophical point of view.

And, in any case, these two, mutually supporting criticisms of Existentialism raise some fundamental issues about the nature of philosophical theorizing. The question of whether there is a level of truth about human beings that does not depend on the socio-historical circumstances of our existence is a live issue in contemporary philosophy. Ironically, the stance of the Existentialists in affirming such a level receives support from a domain of human inquiry whose importance they tended to minimize: the natural sciences. Studies in cognitive science have given new support to the notion that there are fundamental structures of the human mind that are part of our biological make-up. And these structures determine basic features of our existence. Although the Existentialists might have recoiled at the notion that our biology determines fundamental aspects of our lives and experience, they also might have come to recognize the support that their notions could receive from this apparently unlikely companion.

All of this is just to say that, despite fundamental criticisms of the methodology and claims of Existentialism, it remains – or *should* remain – a competitor in the contemporary marketplace of philosophical ideas. No other philosophical point of view provides a better way to focus on important aspects of our lives as human beings. This is because no other school or tradition of philosophical thinking has had as adequate a means for incorporating into its philosophical framework such a wide range of issues about how we live our lives. Certainly, traditional rationalism and empiricism did reflect on certain life issues for human beings, the most central being whether science or religion was a more adequate guide for conducting one's life. But those schools lacked a way to conceptualize other life issues as having broad philosophical significance. And, even when they did, they failed to reflect on those issues with the specificity that is characteristic of the Existentialists' phenomenological approach.

The abiding legacy of Existentialism as a philosophical movement, then, is its treatment of all the issues of human life – birth, death, love, sex, marriage, and so on – as *philosophical* issues. Although these ideas had been recognized to have philosophical significance before the Existentialists – Hegel is the prime example of a philosopher who included such topics in his comprehensive account of human history and society – the Existentialists emphasized the *personal* as well as the *philosophical* nature of these issues. That is, they showed how each of these issues is one that individual human beings have to confront during their lives – or avoid at their peril. They also viewed our responses to these concerns as *individual*, rather than general, as Hegel had supposed. As a result, Existentialism is a philosophical viewpoint that helps us understand our existence as individuals without providing general recipes for how to resolve the questions that we inevitably need to answer in our own lives about such crucial subjects as sexuality, love, and death.

Because they treated these issues as part of the ontological concerns of the human being, the Existentialists bequeathed to philosophy the task of reflecting upon a much broader and more inclusive set of life issues than philosophers had traditionally acknowledged. No longer would it do to relegate concerns such as those concerning our sexuality to the realm of the empirical, as that above which philosophy seeks to rise. Instead, the Existentialists asked philosophy to acknowledge that it had developed a means for a deep and abiding investigation of the significance that such issues have for the lives of human beings, one that supports the individualized way in which each person chooses to answer them.

So even if we wish to reject many of the specific claims made about human beings and their involvement in the world by the Existentialists, we need to acknowledge the importance of their enterprise: to bring into the sphere of philosophical thinking all of the significant concerns of human beings, so that we come to see our own lives and how we live them as having significance from a philosophical point of view. Not only would philosophy thereby return to its honorable roots in the everyday concerns of ordinary human beings about how to live their lives, but we would also be able to see our own lives, commonplace as they seem at times, as having philosophical and Existential import. The result might just be that we would see our own struggles and concerns as weighty and our attempts to solve them, heroic, so that, like Camus and the other Existentialists, we might come to see ourselves as having to face issues and employ psychic resources that are similar to those of the Ancient Greek heroes. And while we might not come to see ourselves as happy in our defiance of the gods – as Camus suggested we would – we might still be empowered to take our lives more seriously as the unique gifts we are so fortunate to possess. In so doing, the Existentialists' hope is to provide us with the intellectual tools that afford us the possibility of constructing meaningful lives for ourselves not by fulfilling some pre-ordained purpose, but by creating ourselves as beings who, in touch with the deepest possibilities of human existence, have realized those possibilities in our own unique and individual ways.

Nothing was more important to the Existentialists than getting human beings to take more advantage of the freedom that they possess. All too often, we tend to act as if our options for living are highly circumscribed. And, of course, sometimes they really are. But many times, we are our own worst enemies, at least in terms of accepting limitations on our hopes and aspirations that no one else has actually imposed on us. The fundamental message that the Existentialists hoped to deliver to us is that we have many more options for living our lives than we typically acknowledge, that we have the ability to be much more than we typically choose to be. In making their case, the Existentialists sought to push us out of the ruts into which our lives so often fall, if for no other reason than the security those well-worn paths appear to offer. But the Existentialists ask us not to be satisfied with taking the easy route, urging us instead to confront our fears and opt for those less-traveled paths we may have to hew for ourselves. After all, this is the one shot you have at life. Why not live it as an Existentialist?

Further reading

Introduction

Camus, Albert. 1953. *The Myth of Sisyphus and Other Essays*, Justin O'Brien, trans. New York: Knopf.

—— 1988. *The Stranger*, Mathew Ward, trans. New York: Knopf.

Sartre, Jean-Paul. 1946. *No Exit and Three Other Plays*. New York: Vintage Books.

—— 1956. 'Existentialism is a Humanism,' in *Existentialism from Dostoevsky to Sartre*, Walter Kaufmann, ed. New York: Meridian, 345–69.

Shakespeare, William. 2003. *Hamlet*. New York: Washington Square Press.

Chapter 1

Dostoevsky, Fyodor. 1960. *Notes From Underground and the Grand Inquisitor*, Ralph E. Matlaw, trans. New York: E.P. Dutton.

Farias, Victor. 1989. *Heidegger and Nazism*. Philadelphia, PA: Temple University Press.

Heidegger, Martin. 1962. *Being and Time*, John Macquarrie and Edward Robinson, trans. San Francisco: Harper.

Husserl, Edmund. 1960. *Cartesian Meditations: An Introduction to Phenomenology*, Dorion Cairns, trans. The Hague: Nijhoff.

—— 1964. *The Phenomenology of Internal Time-Consciousness*, James S. Churchill, trans. Bloomington, IN: University of Indiana Press.

Nietzsche, Friedrich. 1999. *The Birth of Tragedy and Other Writings*, Ronald Spears, trans. Cambridge, UK: Cambridge University Press.

Sartre, Jean-Paul. 1956. 'Existentialism is a Humanism,' in *Existentialism from Dostoevsky to Sartre*, Walter Kaufmann, ed. New York: Meridian, 345–69.
—— 1964. *Nausea*, Lloyd Alexander, trans. Norfolk, CT: New Directions.
—— 1992. *Being and Nothingness: A Phenomenological Essay on Ontology*, Hazel Barnes, trans. New York: Washington Square Press.

Chapter 2

Dostoevsky, Fyodor. 1990. *The Brothers Karamazov*, Richard Pevear and Larissa Volokhonsky, trans. San Francisco: North Point Press.
Fromm, Erich. 1941. *Escape from Freedom*. New York: Farrar and Rinehart.
Hill, David. 1981. *The Gospel of Matthew*. Grand Rapids. MI: William B. Eerdmans Publishing Company.
Sartre, Jean-Paul. 1946. *No Exit and Three Other Plays*. New York: Vintage Books.

Chapter 3

Berkeley, George. 1988. *The Principles of Human Knowledge and Three Dialogues between Hylas and Philonus*. New York: Penguin.
Descartes, René. 1993. *Meditations on First Philosophy*, Donald A. Cress, trans. Indianapolis: Hackett Publishers.
Hegel, G.W.F. 1977. *The Phenomenology of Spirit*, A.V. Miller, trans. Oxford: Clarendon Press.
Heidegger, Martin. 2007. 'The Origin of the Work of Art,' in *The Nature of Art*, Thomas Wartenberg, ed. Belmont, CA: Thomson Wadsworth, 149–70.
Shakespeare, William. 2004. *Othello*. New York: Washington Square Press.

Spinoza, Baruch. 1991. *The Ethics*. Indianapolis: Hackett Publishers.
Wittgenstein, Ludwig. 2003. *The Philosophical Investigations*, G.E.M. Anscombe, trans. Oxford: Blackwell.

Chapter 4

Anselm, Saint of Canterbury. 1998. *The Basic Works*. Oxford: Oxford University Press.

Auden, W.H. 1947. *The Age of Anxiety*. New York: Random House.

Descartes, René. 1993. *Meditations on First Philosophy*, Donald A. Cress, trans. Indianapolis: Hackett Publishers.

Freud, Sigmund. 1991. *Introductory Lectures on Psychoanalysis*. New York: Penguin Books.

Frost, Robert. 2002. *The Poetry of Robert Frost*. New York: Owl Books.

Hume, David. 1980. *Dialogues Concerning Natural Religion*. Indianapolis: Hackett Publishers.

Kant, Immanuel. 1997. *Critique of Pure Reason*, Paul Guyer and Allen W. Wood, trans. Cambridge, UK: Cambridge University Press.

Kierkegaard, Søren. 1983. *Fear and Trembling/Repetition*, Howard V. Hong and Edna H. Hong, trans. Princeton, NJ: Princeton University Press.

Sartre, Jean-Paul. 1992. *Being and Nothingness : A Phenomenological Essay on Ontology*. Hazel Estella Barnes, trans. New York: Washington Square Press.

Chapter 5

Aristotle. 1962. *The Nichomachean Ethics*, Martin Ostwald, trans. Indianapolis: Bobbs-Merrill Educational Publishing.

Dostoevsky, Fyodor. 1990. *The Brothers Karamazov*, Richard Pevear and Larissa Volokhonsky, trans. San Francisco: North Point Press.

Heidegger, Martin. 1962. *Being and Time*, John Macquarrie and Edward Robinson, trans. San Francisco: Harper.

Kant, Immanuel. 1997. *Critique of Pure Reason*, Paul Guyer and Allen W. Wood, trans. Cambridge, UK: Cambridge University Press.

Leibniz, Gottfried. 1985. *Theodicy*. Chicago: Open Court.

Plato. 1993. *The Last Days of Socrates; Euthyphro; The Apology; Crito; Phaedo*, Hugh Tredennick, trans. New York: Penguin.

Tolstoy, Leo. 2003. *The Death of Ivan Ilych and Other Stories*. New York: Signet.

Voltaire. 1950. *Candide: Or Optimism*, John Butt, trans. New York: Penguin.

Chapter 6

Beckett, Samuel. 1954. *Waiting for Godot: A Tragicomedy in Two Acts*. New York: Grove Press.

Camus, Albert. 1953. *The Myth of Sisyphus and Other Essays*, Justin O'Brien, trans. New York: Knopf.

Kafka, Franz. 2005. *The Trial*. New York: Vintage Books.

Nagel, Thomas. 1971. 'The Absurd,' *The Journal of Philosophy*. 68. 716–27.

Sartre, Jean-Paul. 1946. *The Flies* in *No Exit and Three Other Plays*. New York: Vintage Books.

—— 1956. 'Existentialism is a Humanism,' in *Existentialism from Dostoevsky to Sartre*, Walter Kaufmann, ed. New York: Meridian. 345–69.

Sophocles. 1996. *The Oedipus Plays of Sophocles*, Paul Roche, trans. New York: Plume.

Chapter 7

de Beauvoir, Simone. 1948. *The Ethics of Ambiguity*, Bernard Frechtman, trans. Secaucus, NJ: Citadel Press.

Heidegger, Martin. 1962. *Being and Time*, John Macquarrie and Edward Robinson, trans. San Francisco: Harper.

Nietzsche, Friedrich. 2006. *Thus Spake Zarathustra: A Book for All and None*, Adrian Del Caro and Robert B. Pippin, trans. Cambridge, UK: Cambridge University Press.

Plato. 1993. *The Last Days of Socrates; Euthyphro; The Apology; Crito; Phaedo*, Hugh Tredennick, trans. New York: Penguin.

Sartre, Jean-Paul. 1956. 'Existentialism is a Humanism,' in *Existentialism from Dostoevsky to Sartre*, Walter Kaufmann, ed. New York: Meridian, 345–69.

Tolstoy, Leo. 2003. *The Death of Ivan Ilych and Other Stories*. New York: Signet.

Chapter 8

de Beauvoir, Simone. 1989. *The Second Sex*, H.M. Parshley, trans. New York: Vintage Books.

Fanon, Frantz. 1963. *The Wretched of the Earth*, Constance Farrington, trans. New York: Grove Weidenfeld.

—— 1967. *Black Skin, White Masks*, Charles Lam Markmann, trans. New York, Grove Press

Sartre, Jean-Paul. 1965. *Anti-Semite and Jew*, George J. Becker, trans. New York: Shocken Books.

Shaw, George Bernard. 1957. *Pygmalion*. London: Penguin.

Chapter 9

There are lots of theories and ideas put forward by the Existentialists that I have not been able to discuss in this *Beginner's Guide*. So, for example, I passed over in silence such important Existentialists as Martin Buber (1878–1965) and Karl Jaspers (1883–1969), and the contributions they made to the Existentialist Tradition. Buber was a religious Existentialist who emphasized the importance of non-alienated human relationships, what he termed 'I–Thou' relationships. He also advocated an evolutionary form of socialism, modeled in part on the *kibbutzim* in Israel. Jaspers stressed the importance of transcendence in his writings, our quest as limited beings for knowledge that goes beyond its inevitable boundaries. On the basis of this idea, he developed a philosophy of *Existenz* that emphasized the standard Existentialist themes of freedom and possibility.

There are also many important themes to which I was not able to give sufficient attention in this primer to the subject. Although I mentioned Maurice Merleau-Ponty, I wasn't able to discuss his important work on the nature of perception nor show the significance of his systematic attack on the mind–body dualism in Western thought. If you are interested in these topics, his two books *The Visible and the Invisible* (1989) and *The Structure of Behaviour* (1963) are still widely available and rewarding reads. And even in regard to a thinker I spent a great deal of time discussing, Jean-Paul Sartre, I had to ignore some of his important claims and theories. For example, although I briefly discussed Sartre's fascinating investigation of the different ways in which we attempt to 'take back' our selves from the other's alienating look, I didn't have sufficient time to discuss all the different forms that this effort took, and how each dialectically turned into another form. A great deal also could be learned by taking a more extended look at Sartre's discussion of such modes of human relationship as love and sadism. He discusses these and other topics in the chapter 'Concrete Relations with Others' in *Being and Nothingness* (471–556). In addition, I left aside the vexed question of the relationship between Marxism and Existentialism, a topic to which Sartre, among others, devoted a great deal of attention. Indeed, his reflections on this issue account for the constant evolution that his thought underwent during his lifetime, as he tried to accommodate the weight of facticity, both individual and social, into his thought.

Buber, Martin. 1988. *I and Thou*, Walter Kaufmann, trans. New York: MacMillan.

Habermas, Jürgen. 1990. *The Philosophical Discourse of Modernity*, Frederick G. Lawrence, trans. Cambridge, MA: MIT Press.

Jaspers, Karl. 1971. *The Philosophy of Existence*, Richard F. Grabau, trans. Philadelphia: University of Pennsylvania Press.

Merleau-Ponty, Maurice. 1963. *The Structure of Behavior*. Alden L. Fisher, trans. Boston, MA: Beacon Press.

—— 1989. *The Visible and the Invisible*. Alphonso Lingis, trans. Evanston, IL: Northwestern University Press.

Sartre, Jean-Paul. 1992. *Being and Nothingness : A Phenomenological Essay on Ontology*. Hazel Estella Barnes, trans. New York: Washington Square Press.

Bibliography

Anselm, Saint of Canterbury. 1998. *The Basic Works*. Oxford: Oxford University Press.

Arendt, Hannah. 1998. *The Human Condition*. 2nd ed. Chicago: University of Chicago Press.

Aristotle. 1962. *The Nichomachean Ethics*, Martin Ostwald, trans. Indianapolis: Bobbs-Merrill Educational Publishing.

Aron, Raymond. 1969. *Marxism and the Existentialists*. New York: Harper & Row.

Auden, W.H. 1947. *The Age of Anxiety*. New York: Random House.

Barnes, Hazel E. 1967. *An Existentialist Ethics*. New York: Knopf.

Barrett, William. 1962. *Irrational Man: A Study in Existential Philosophy*. Garden City, NJ: Doubleday.

Beckett, Samuel. 1954. *Waiting for Godot: A Tragicomedy in Two Acts*. New York: Grove Press.

Berkeley, George. 1988. *The Principles of Human Knowledge and Three Dialogues between Hylas and Philonus*. New York: Penguin.

Buber, Martin. 1948. *Between Man and Man*. Ronald Gregor Smith, trans. New York: Macmillan.

—— 1988. *I and Thou*. Walter Arnold Kaufmann, trans. New York: Macmillan.

Butler, Judith. 1990. *Gender Trouble: Feminism and the Subversion of Identity*. New York: Routledge.

Camus, Albert. 1953. *The Myth of Sisyphus, and Other Essays*. Justin O'Brien, trans. New York: Knopf.

—— 1957. *The Fall*. Justin O'Brien, trans. New York: Knopf.

—— 1962. *Caligula and Three Other Plays*. Stuart Gilbert, trans. New York: Vintage Books.

—— 1988. *The Stranger*. Matthew Ward, trans. New York: Knopf.

—— 1991. *The Rebel: An Essay on Man in Revolt*. Anthony Bower, trans. New York: Vintage Books.

* —— 2001. *The Plague*. Robin Buss, trans. London: Allen Lane.

Cavell, Stanley. 1969. *Must We Mean What We Say?* New York: Scribner.

Caws, Peter. 1979. *Sartre*. London: Routledge.

Collins, James D. 1952. *The Existentialists, a Critical Study*. Chicago: H. Regnery.

Cooper, David E. 1999. *Existentialism: A Reconstruction*. 2nd ed. Oxford: Blackwell.

Crowell, Steven G. 2001. *Husserl, Heidegger, and the Space of Meaning: Paths Toward Transcendental Phenomenology*. Evanston, IL: Northwestern University Press.

Danto, Arthur C. 1975. *Jean-Paul Sartre*. New York: Viking Press.

—— 1980. *Nietzsche as Philosopher*. New York: Columbia University Press.

de Beauvoir, Simone. 1948. *The Ethics of Ambiguity*. Bernard Frechtman, trans. Secausus, NJ: Citadel Press.

—— 1960. *The Mandarins*. Leonard M. Friedman, trans. London: Fontana Paperbacks.

—— 1972. *The Coming of Age*. Patrick O'Brian, trans. New York: Putnam.

—— 1989. *The Second Sex*. H.M. Parshley, trans. New York: Vintage Books.

Descartes, René. 1993. *Meditations on First Philosophy*, Donald A. Cress, trans. Indianapolis: Hackett Publishers.

de Unamuno, Miguel. 1954. *Tragic Sense of Life*. J.E. Crawford Flitch, trans. New York: Dover Publications.

Dostoevsky, Fyodor. 1916. *The Possessed: A Novel in Three Parts*. Constance Garnett, trans. New York: Macmillan.

—— 1960. *Notes from Underground and the Grand Inquisitor*, Ralph E. Matlaw, trans. New York: E.P. Dutton.

—— 1990. *The Brothers Karamazov*, Richard Pevear and Larissa Volokhonsky, trans. San Francisco: North Point Press.

—— 1995. *Crime and Punishment*. Jessie Coulson, trans. New York: Oxford University Press.

—— 2004. *The Idiot*. David McDuff, trans. London: Penguin Books.

Dreyfus, Hubert L. 1979. *What Computers can't do: The Limits of Artificial Intelligence*. New York: Harper & Row.

—— 1991. *Being-in-the-World: A Commentary on Heidegger's* Being and Time*, Division I*. Cambridge, MA: MIT Press.

Dreyfus, Hubert L., and Hall, Harrison, eds. 1992. *Heidegger : a critical reader*. Oxford: Blackwell.

• Dreyfus, Hubert L., and Wathall, Mark A., eds. 2006. *A Companion to Phenomenology and Existentialism*. Oxford: Blackwell.

Fackenheim, Emil L. 1961. *Metaphysics and Historicity*. Milwaukee, WI: Marquette University Press.

Fanon, Frantz. 1963. *The Wretched of the Earth*. Constance Farrington, trans. New York: Grove Weidenfeld.

—— 1967. *Black Skin, White Masks*. Charles Lam Markmann, trans. New York: Grove Press.

• Farias, Victor. 1989. *Heidegger and Nazism*. Philadelphia, Temple University Press.

Fell, Joseph P. 1979. *Heidegger and Sartre: An Essay on Being and Place*. New York: Columbia University Press.

Flynn, Thomas R. 1997. *Sartre, Foucault, and Historical Reason*. Chicago: University of Chicago Press.

Freud, Sigmund. 1991. *Introductory Lectures on Psychoanalysis*. New York: Penguin Books.

Fromm, Erich. 1941. *Escape from Freedom*. New York: Farrar and Rinehart.

Frost, Robert. 2002. *The Poetry of Robert Frost*. New York: Owl Books.

Gardiner, Patrick L. 1988. *Kierkegaard*. Oxford: Oxford University Press.

Golomb, Jacob. 1995. *In Search of Authenticity*. London: Routledge.

Gordon, Lewis R. 1995. *Bad Faith and Antiblack Racism*. Atlantic Highlands, NJ: Humanities Press.

—— 2000. *Existentia Africana: Understanding Africana Existential Thought*. New York: Routledge.

Grene, Marjorie G. 1948. *Dreadful Freedom, a Critique of Existentialism.* Chicago: University of Chicago Press.

Guignon, Charles B., ed. 1983. *Heidegger and the Problem of Knowledge.* Indianapolis: Hackett.

—— 1993. *The Cambridge Companion to Heidegger.* Cambridge, UK: Cambridge University Press.

Guignon, Charles B., and Pereboom, Derk, eds. 2001. *Existentialism: Basic Writings.* 2nd ed. Indianapolis: Hackett.

Habermas, Jürgen. 1990. *The Philosophical Discourse of Modernity,* Frederick G. Lawrence, trans. Cambridge, MA: MIT Press.

Hannay, Alastair. 1982. *Kierkegaard.* London: Routledge.

Hegel, G.W.F. 1977. *Phenomenology of Spirit.* Arnold V. Miller, trans. Oxford: Clarendon Press.

—— 1990. *Encyclopedia of the Philosophical Sciences in Outline, and Critical Writings.* Ernst Behler, ed. Arnold V. Miller, trans. New York: Continuum.

Heidegger, Martin. 1962. *Being and Time.* John Macquarrie and Edward Robinson, trans. San Francisco: Harper.

—— 1971. *Poetry, Language, Thought.* Albert Hofstadter, trans. New York: Harper & Row.

—— 1977. 'Letter on Humanism,' in *Basic Writings*, David Farrell Krell, ed. New York: Harper & Row.

—— 2007. 'The Origin of the Work of Art,' in *The Nature of Art*, Thomas Wartenberg, ed. Belmont, CA: Thomson Wadsworth, 149–70.

Higgins, Kathleen M. 1987. *Nietzsche's Zarathustra.* Philadelphia: Temple University Press.

Hill, David. 1981. *The Gospel of Matthew.* Grand Rapids. MI: William B. Eerdmans Publishing Company.

Hume, David. 1980. *Dialogues Concerning Natural Religion.* Indianapolis: Hackett Publishers.

Husserl, Edmund. 1931. *Ideas: General Introduction to Pure Phenomenology.* William Ralph Boyce Gibson, trans. New York: Macmillan.

—— 1960. *Cartesian Meditations: An Introduction to Phenomenology.* Dorion Cairns, trans. The Hague: Nijhoff.

—— 1964. *The Phenomenology of Internal Time-Consciousness*. James S. Churchill, trans. Bloomington, IN: University of Indiana Press.

Jaspers, Karl. 1955. *Reason and Existenz; Five Lectures*. William Earle, trans. New York: Noonday Press.

—— 1971. *The Philosophy of Existence*, Richard F. Grabau, trans. Philadelphia: University of Pennsylvania Press.

Judt, Tony. 1992. *Past Imperfect: French Intellectuals, 1944–1956*. Berkeley: University of California Press.

Kafka, Franz. 2005. *The Trial*. New York: Vintage Books.

Kant, Immanuel. 1997. *Critique of Practical Reason*. Mary J. Gregor, ed. Cambridge, UK: Cambridge University Press.

—— 1997. *Critique of Pure Reason*. Paul Guyer and Allen W. Wood, trans. Cambridge, UK: Cambridge University Press.

—— 2007. *Critique of Judgement*. Nicholas Walker, ed. James Creed Meredith, trans. Oxford: Oxford University Press.

Kaufmann, Walter A. 1956. *Existentialism from Dostoevsky to Sartre*. New York: Meridian Books.

—— 1974. *Nietzsche: Philosopher, Psychologist, Antichrist*. 4th ed. Princeton, NJ: Princeton University Press.

Kierkegaard, Søren. 1962. *Philosophical Fragments; Or, a Fragment of Philosophy*. 2nd ed. David F. Swenson and Howard Vincent Hong, trans. Princeton, NJ: Princeton University Press.

—— 1983. *Fear and Trembling/Repetition*. Howard Vincent Hong and Edna Hatlestad Hong, trans. Princeton, NJ: Princeton University Press.

—— 1987. *Either/Or: A Fragment of Life*. Edna Hatlestad Hong and Howard Vincent Hong, trans. Princeton, NJ: Princeton University Press.

—— 1992. *Concluding Unscientific Postscript to Philosophical Fragments*. Edna Hatlestad Hong and Howard Vincent Hong, trans. Princeton, NJ: Princeton University Press.

Kruks, Sonia. 1990. *Situation and Human Existence: Freedom, Subjectivity, and Society*. London: Unwin Hyman.

Leibniz, Gottfried W. 1985. *Theodicy*. Chicago: Open Court.

Macquarrie, John. 1972. *Existentialism*. London: Hutchinson.

Marcel, Gabriel. 1949. *Being and Having*. Katharine Farrer, trans. Westminster: Dacre Press.

McBride, William L. 1991. *Sartre's Political Theory*. Bloomington: University of Indiana Press.

—— 1997. *The Development and Meaning of Twentieth-Century Existentialism*. New York: Garland.

Merleau–Ponty, Maurice. 1962. *Phenomenology of Perception*. Colin Smith, trans. New York: Humanities Press.

—— 1963. *The Structure of Behavior*. Alden L. Fisher, trans. Boston, MA: Beacon Press.

—— 1973. *Adventures of the Dialectic*. Joseph Bien, trans. Evanston, IL : Northwestern University Press.

—— 1989. *The Visible and the Invisible*. Alphonso Lingis, trans. Evanston, IL: Northwestern University Press.

Moran, Richard. 2001. *Authority and Estrangement: An Essay on Self-Knowledge*. Princeton, NJ: Princeton University Press.

Murray, Michael, ed. 1978. *Heidegger and Modern Philosophy: Critical Essays*. New Haven, CT: Yale University Press.

Nagel, Thomas. 1971. 'The Absurd,' *The Journal of Philosophy*. 68. 716–27.

—— 1979. *Mortal Questions*. Cambridge, UK: Cambridge University Press.

Nehamas, Alexander. 1985. *Nietzsche, Life as Literature*. Cambridge, MA: Harvard University Press.

—— 1998. *The Art of Living: Socratic Reflections from Plato to Foucault*. Berkeley: University of California Press.

Nietzsche, Friedrich W. 1966. *Beyond Good and Evil*. Walter Arnold Kaufmann, trans. New York: Vintage Books.

—— 1967. *The Will to Power*. Walter Arnold Kaufmann and R.J. Hollingdale, trans. New York: Random House.

—— 1969. *On the Genealogy of Morals*. Walter Arnold Kaufmann, trans. New York: Vintage Books.

—— 1974. *The Gay Science; with a Prelude in Rhymes and an Appendix of Songs*. Walter Arnold Kaufmann, trans. New York: Vintage Books.

—— 1998. *Twilight of the Idols, Or, how to Philosophize with a Hammer.* Duncan Large, trans. Oxford: Oxford University Press.

—— 1999. *The Birth of Tragedy and Other Writings.* Ronald Spears, trans. Cambridge, UK: Cambridge University Press.

—— 2006. *Thus Spake Zarathustra : A Book for all and None.* Adrian Del Caro and Robert B. Pippin, trans. Cambridge, UK: Cambridge University Press.

Olafson, Frederick A. 1967. *Principles and Persons; an Ethical Interpretation of Existentialism.* Baltimore, MD: Johns Hopkins Press.

—— 1987. *Heidegger and the Philosophy of Mind.* New Haven, CT: Yale University Press.

—— 1998. *Heidegger and the Ground of Ethics: A Study of Mitsein.* Cambridge, UK: Cambridge University Press.

Ortega y Gasset, José. 1985. *The Revolt of the Masses.* Kenneth Moore, ed. Anthony Kerrigan, trans. Notre Dame, IN: University of Notre Dame Press.

Plato. 1993. *The Last Days of Socrates; Euthyphro; The Apology; Crito; Phaedo.* Hugh Tredennick, trans. New York: Penguin.

Poster, Mark. 1975. *Existential Marxism in Postwar France: From Sartre to Althusser.* Princeton, NJ: Princeton University Press.

Sartre, Jean-Paul. 1946. *No Exit and Three Other Plays.* New York: Vintage Books.

—— 1956. 'Existentialism is a Humanism,' in *Existentialism from Dosteovsky to Sartre*, Walter Arnold Kaufmann, ed. New York: Meridian, 345–69.

—— 1963. *Saint Genet: Actor and Martyr.* Bernard Frechtman, trans. New York: G. Braziller.

—— 1964. *Nausea.* Lloyd Alexander, trans. New York: New Directions.

—— 1965. *Anti-Semite and Jew*, George J. Becker, trans. New York: Shocken Books.

—— 1968. *Search for a Method.* Hazel Estella Barnes, trans. New York: Vintage Books.

—— 1975. *The Words.* Bernard Frechtman, trans. Greenwich: Fawcett Publications.

—— 1976. *Critique of Dialectical Reason*. Alan Sheridan-Smith, trans. London: Nlb.

—— 1981. *The Family Idiot: Gustave Flaubert, 1821–1857*. Carol Cosman, trans. Chicago: University of Chicago Press.

—— 1988. *'What is Literature?' and Other Essays*. Cambridge, MA: Harvard University Press.

—— 1992. *Being and Nothingness : A Phenomenological Essay on Ontology*. Hazel Estella Barnes, trans. New York: Washington Square Press.

Schacht, Richard. 1983. *Nietzsche*. London: Routledge.

Schilpp, Paul A., ed. 1981. *The Philosophy of Jean-Paul Sartre*. LaSalle, IL: Open Court.

Schilpp, Paul A., and Friedman, Maurice S., eds. 1967. *The Philosophy of Martin Buber*. LaSalle: Open Court.

Schilpp, Paul A., and Jaspers, Karl, eds. 1957. *The Philosophy of Karl Jaspers*. New York: Tudor.

Shakespeare, William. 2003. *Hamlet*. New York: Washington Square Press.

—— 2004. *Othello*. New York: Washington Square Press.

Shaw, George Bernard. 1957. *Pygmalion*. London: Penguin.

Sheehan, Thomas, ed. 1981. *Heidegger, The Man and the Thinker*. Chicago: Precedent.

Shestov, Lev. 1969. *Kierkegaard and the Existential Philosophy*. Elinor Hewitt, trans. Athens: Ohio University Press.

Solomon, Robert C. 1972. *From Rationalism to Existentialism: The Existentialists and their Nineteenth-Century Backgrounds*. New York: Harper & Row.

—— 1987. *From Hegel to Existentialism*. New York: Oxford University Press.

—— 1988. *Continental Philosophy since 1750: The Rise and Fall of the Self*. Oxford: Oxford University Press.

Sophocles. 1996. *The Oedipus Plays of Sophocles*, Paul Roche, trans. New York: Plume.

Spiegelberg, Herbert, and Schuhmann, Karl. 1982. *The Phenomenological Movement: A Historical Introduction*. The Hague: Nijhoff.

Spinoza, Baruch. 1991. *The Ethics*. Indianapolis: Hackett Publishers.

Stewart, Jon, ed. 1998. *The Debate between Sarte and Merleau-Ponty*. Evanston, IL: Northwestern University Press.

Taylor, Charles. 1989. *Sources of the Self: The Making of the Modern Identity*. Cambridge, MA: Harvard University Press.

Tillich, Paul. 2000. *The Courage to be*. 2nd ed. New Haven, CT: Yale University Press.

Tolstoy, Leo. 1995. *What is Art?* Richard Pevear and Larissa Volokhonsky, trans. London: Penguin.

—— 1999. *Anna Karenina*. Aylmer Maude and Louise Shanks Maude, trans. Oxford: Oxford University Press.

—— 2003. *The Death of Ivan Ilych and Other Stories*. New York: Signet.

—— 2006. *War and Peace*. Anthony Briggs, trans. New York: Viking.

Voltaire. 1950. *Candide: Or Optimism*, John Butt, trans. New York: Penguin.

Wahl, Jean A. 1949. *A Short History of Existentialism*. Forrest Williams and Stanley Maron, trans. New York: Philosophical Library.

—— 1969. *Philosophies of Existence; an Introduction to the Basic Thought of Kierkegaard, Heidegger, Jaspers, Marcel, Sartre*. F.M. Lory, trans. New York: Schocken Books.

Warnock, Mary. 1965. *The Philosophy of Sartre*. London: Hutchinson University Library.

—— 1967. *Existentialist Ethics*. London: Macmillan.

—— 1970. *Existentialism*. London: Oxford University Press.

Wild, John D. 1955. *The Challenge of Existentialism*. Bloomington: Indiana University Press.

Wittgenstein, Ludwig. 2003. *The Philosophical Investigations*, G.E.M. Anscombe, trans. Oxford: Blackwell.

Zaner, Richard M., and Ihde, Don. 1973. *Phenomenology and Existentialism*. New York: Putnam.

Filmography

The following list contains films that, in one way or another, present the ideas of Existentialism. I make no claims for completeness. Nor do I vouch for the quality of every film included.

13 Conversations about One Thing (Jill Sprecher, 2001)
A bout de souffle (*Breathless*) (Jean-Luc Godard, 1960)
Addiction, The (Abel Ferrara, 1995)
Alphaville, une étrange aventure de Lemmy Caution (Jean-Luc Godard, 1965)
American Beauty (Sam Mendes, 1999)
Annie Hall (Woody Allen, 1977)
Apocalypse Now (Francis Ford Coppola, 1979)
Babette's Feast (Gabriel Axel, 1987)
Baisers volés (*Stolen Kisses*) (Francois Truffaut, 1968)
Being There (Hal Ashby, 1979)
Big Lebowski, The (Joel and Ethan Coen, 1998)
Casablanca (Michael Curtiz, 1942)
Clockwork Orange, A (Stanley Kubrick, 1971)
Conversations with God (Stephen Simon, 2006)
Crimes and Misdemeanors (Woody Allen, 1988)
Crimson Tide (Tony Scott, 1995)
Cross of Iron (Sam Peckinpah, 1977)
Cutter's Way (Ivan Passer, 1981)
Doctor, The (Thomas Nola, 2005)
Donnie Darko (Richard Kelly, 2001)
Easy Rider (Dennis Hopper, 1969)
Electra Glide in Blue (James William Guercio, 1973)
Falling Down (Joel Schumacher, 1993)
Fight Club (David Fincher, 1999)

Flower Thief, The (Ron Rice, 1960)

Forrest Gump (Robert Zemeckis, 1994)

Frantz Fanon: Black Skin, White Mask (Isaac Julien, 1995)

High Noon (Fred Zinnemann, 1952)

I Heart Huckabees (David O. Russell, 2004)

I Sequestrati di Altona (*The Condemned of Altona*) (Vittorio de Sica, 1963)

Ikiru (Akira Kurosawa, 1952)

L'eclisse (*The Eclipse*) (Michelangelo Antonioni, 1962)

La Peste (*The Plague*) (Luis Puenzo, 1992)

Le Mari de la coiffeuse (*The Hairdresser's Husband*) (Patrice Leconte, 1990)

Le Notti bianche (*White Nights*) (Luchino Visconti, 1957)

Les Enfants du Paradis (*Children of Paradise*) (Marcel Carne, 1945)

Les Miserables (Bille August, 1998)

Leaving Las Vegas (Mike Figgis, 1995)

Lost in Translation (Sofia Coppola, 2003)

Love and Death (Woody Allen, 1975)

Machinist, The (Brad Anderson, 2004)

Matrix, The (Andy and Larry Wachowski, 1999)

Matrix Reloaded, The (Andy and Larry Wachowski, 2003)

Matrix Revolutions (Andy and Larry Wachowski, 2003)

Mechanic, The (Michael Winner, 1972)

My Dinner with Andre (Louis Malle, 1981)

My Life Without Me (Isabel Coixet, 2003)

Nobody's Fool (Robert Benton, 1994)

Notes from Underground (Gary Walkow, 1995)

Ordinary People (Robert Redford, 1980)

Out of Africa (Sydney Pollack, 1985)

Persona (Ingmar Bergman, 1966)

Professione: reporter (*The Passenger*) (Michelangelo Antonioni, 1975)

Pull My Daisy (Robert Frank and Alfred Leslie, 1959)

Rosencrantz and Guildenstern are Dead (Tom Stoppard, 1990)

Rules of Attraction, The (Roger Avary, 2002)

Sartre par lui-meme (*Sartre by Himself*) (Alexandre Astruc and Michel Contat, 1989)

Seventh Seal, The (Ingmar Bergman, 1957)

Simone de Beauvoir (Malka Ribowska and Josée Dayan, 1978)
Stranger Than Fiction (Marc Forster, 2006)
Suddenly, Last Summer (Joseph L. Mankiewicz, 1959)
Taxi Driver (Martin Scorsese, 1976)
Unbearable Lightness of Being, The (Philip Kaufman, 1988)
Vanishing Point (Richard C. Sarafian, 1971)
Vertigo (Alfred Hitchcock, 1958)
Waking Life (Richard Linklater, 2001)
Wild Strawberries (Ingmar Bergman, 1957)
Wit (Mike Nichols, 2001)

Index

Note: Entries in **Bold** refer to text boxes.

A Beginner's Guide to
Postmodernism

Kevin Hart steers a steady course through the pitfalls and perplexities of postmodernism, revealing the true 'meaning' (if such a thing exists) of this elusive concept.

978-1-85168-338-3 | £9.99

"Hart's book moves easily, wittily, and informatively over an impressive range of phenomena – cultural, literary, philosophical, and theological. An unqualified success. " **John D. Caputo**, David R. Cook Professor of Philosophy, Villanova University

"Invaluable: deserves the attention of all serious students of post-modernity." **David Tracy**, Professor of Theology and the Philosophy of Religion in the Divinity School, University of Chicago

"Immensely useful, enabling us to gain, because of its clarity and incisiveness, a broad overview of a complex international development." **Geoffrey Hartman**, Sterling Professor emeritus of
English and Comparative Literature, Yale University

KEVIN HART is Professor of English at the University of Notre Dame, Illinois. He is the author or editor of 15 books, and has published seven collections of poetry, the most recent of which is *Flame Tree: Selected Poems*

Browse further titles at
www.oneworld-publications.com

A Beginner's Guide to
The Brain

978-1-85168-594-3 | £9.99

Using the very latest research in neuroscience this lively introduction explains how 1.4kg of wet grey tissue can not only control all of our bodily functions, thoughts and behaviours, but also house the very essence of who we are.

"A virtuoso performance! The book is technical, easy to read and entertaining." **Garth Nicholson**, Associate Professor of Medical Genetics, University of Sydney

"A concise primer that summarizes the fascinating complexity of the brain in a memorable and refreshingly graspable manner." **Robert Brown**, Professor of Neurology, Harvard Medical School

AMMAR AL-CHALABI is Honorary Consultant Neurologist at King's College Hospital and a Senior Lecturer at King's College London.

MARTIN R. TURNER is a Specialist Registrar in Neurology at the John Radcliffe Hospital in Oxford, and a Clinical Tutorial Fellow at Green College, Oxford University.

R. SHANE DELAMONT is a Consultant Neurologist at King's College Hospital.

Browse further titles at
www.oneworld-publications.com

Beginners
GUIDES